Praise for June and Jim Spencer and *No Bad Feelings!*

"I've applied your philosophy for years with great success. This book is really reader-friendly and offers your unique training to everyone."
—**Kathlene Sebastian, Ph.D.,**
Clinical Psychologist

"June and Jim helped save my life. They are the most exceptional people I've ever met. They live what they teach with great integrity."
—**Sherrie Villano,**
Inter-Faith Minister and Counselor

"Finally, a book that actually helps you understand, accept and love all of your feelings. This could alleviate so much self-created suffering. You have shown us how every person can relate comfortably to all feelings. The freedom and joy that brings is astounding."
—**Francesca James,**
Award-Winning Executive Producer
for ABC Daytime TV

"Let June and Jim Spencer guide you in accomplishing an emotional adjustment which will bring more pleasure into your personal and professional life."
—**Arlene Shovald, Ph.D.,**
Transpersonal Psychotherapist and Author

"*No Bad Feelings!* goes beyond description. Living it has freed me. It is that simple. Now with great joy I am taking it into the corporate world, building truly empowered teams through the expression of feelings."
—**Elizabeth Botta Grandinetti,**
Director, Human Resources

"Distinguishing between pain and the suffering caused by fighting our own feelings comes into play every day at the hospital. I know of no other approach to feelings that is as clear, dependable and helpful as yours. Bless you."
—**Kate Fagan,**
Rabbinic Chaplain

"No Bad Feelings! is a truly indispensable guide to learning how to make peace with all your feelings, the ones you like and the ones you don't. Practical wisdom appears on every page."

—Jennifer Bassie,
Award-Winning Actress,
aka Marian Colby Chandler on
All My Children

"I've led corporate trainings for years and have never seen a system that supports the feelings of the people. Without addressing feelings, any business plan will regress when emotions step in. Your book should be required reading for every businessperson."

—Robert Spencer,
Institute for Human Development

"Health is a multi-level phenomenon. Your insights into emotional health are challenging, unique and thought-provoking."

—Tom Wenger, M.D.

"You guys saved my life! I don't really understand all of it, but it helped pull me through a really @#$%&: time."

—Steve Harris,
Harley Hog and Studio Musician

"The market goes up and down, but because of your guidance I've learned my emotions don't have to. Your chapter 'There's Nothing Out There (Or If I Had a Million Dollars I'd Feel Great)' kept me sailing through the crises for days."

—Richard Erlanger,
Wall Street, Corporate Operations

"You've done it again. I turn to your insights when nothing else is working—and always find relief. The chapter on Connecting is pure brilliance. This helps me with the characters I create as well as the characters I deal with in everyday life."

—Alan Douglas, Ph.D.,
Bodyworker, Inventor, and Playwright

"This book can make such a difference in the lives of so many. Every 12-stepper should read the chapter on Addictions and Aversions. Thank you for giving me a new perspective that works when old emotional patterns resurface."

—David,
Recovering Alcoholic

Best Wishes,
Jim & June

No Bad Feelings!

A Revolutionary Way of Relating to Your Emotions

June and Jim Spencer

Let Go and Live Institute, Ltd.
NATHROP, COLORADO

First printing 2002

ISBN 1-878588-10-9

LCCN 2001130611

ATTENTION CORPORATIONS, UNIVERSITIES, COLLEGES, AND PROFESSIONAL ORGANIZATIONS: Quantity discounts are available on bulk purchases of this book for educational, gift purposes, or as premiums for increasing magazine subscriptions or renewals. Special books or book excerpts can also be created to fit specific needs. For information, please contact Let Go and Live Institute, Ltd., 13060 Elk Run, Nathrop, CO 81236; ph 719-539-3232.

This book is dedicated to all those who have the curiosity and courage to change their minds. It's a blueprint for enjoyment and peace of mind, built on going toward what we want, rather than avoiding what we don't—running to the angels rather than from the goblins.

TABLE OF CONTENTS

✦ ✦ ✦

— PART II —

— PART III —

INTRODUCTION

✦ ✦ ✦

This book is an adventure in *applied philosophy*. The body of the book is the philosophy, yet the application brings it to life. If it were just philosophy, you could read it and decide if you agree or not and perhaps have some wonderful inner debates about its validity. That is a *head experience;* this material is meant to stimulate a *heart experience.*

One of the biggest surprises of this book is that whether you agree with what is being presented or not is of very little importance. Following along to see an application that can benefit your life, however, is of great importance.

We are going to delve into feelings. The end result will show you new ways to live a happier, healthier life that nurtures your spirit. You can't live a new life with the same old perceptions. In order to show you some new angles on old situations, we are going to ask you to change your view on some basic things. This "paradigm shift" is always difficult at first, then eye-opening. The new paradigm is not as important as what it can show you. So, debating the validity of the new paradigm is like debating the ultimate correctness of driving in the right-hand lane or driving in the left-hand lane. Learn to do both and you can safely experience what both the United Kingdom and the rest of the world have to offer.

As Americans we all know that French food, with its fatty sauces can lead to health problems. However, the French go on enjoying their food with fewer coronary problems than we "low-cholesterol" Americans. Shift your paradigm and see what you can discover! "When in Rome, do as the Romans." When in Tuscany, experience a new paradigm. Take a long nap in the heat of the day and then have dinner at midnight with the locals. Or walk through the heat, be upset the stores aren't open, then demand dinner at 5:30 P.M. and go to bed at 10:00 P.M. just as you would at home You'll miss the experience of Tuscany. Of course, if you come from Europe to small-town America and take a long siesta, then go looking for a restaurant at 10:00 P.M., you will be equally out of the loop.

It's hard to get a new outlook from the same old perspective, especially a new outlook regarding your feelings. In order to find a new outlook that can bring greater joy, freedom and understanding, you must be *willing* to explore new paradigms. In Chapter 1, we will examine how life looks if we consider that "all human behavior is built on feelings." Chapter 2 introduces a new paradigm of "feelings come in pairs, and you can't have one without the other." Think of the alternatives that these open up to us.

As we go through the book, we will add some "coaching" notes as we come to these paradigm shifts. Remember that the reward is what you can glean from a new angle, rather than a study of the angle itself. Later, we will come to a new paradigm of "the situation does not create the feelings...what feelings I bring to the situation create my perception of it." Well, as one editor argued, I know someone who was abused as a child and that created feeling patterns that are still strong today. Fine. But if you move into the new paradigm, you get to also see that the past abuse is past.

The focus is, "How can I see this very moment in a new light, so I don't endlessly repeat old reactions I didn't like experiencing in the first place?" This allows an angle of, "I am empowered in this moment to view it from a freer place and shape a present and future that serve me better than my past."

Some people want to debate whether the child was or was not responsible for the past perspective. The question we pose is, "And what good does that head trip do for resolving a heart-felt experience now?"

We will present a system that divides all feelings into four basic categories. Whether it is four categories or seven is not important; however, the results you get from applying the idea are important. Whether a psychologist uses a system of "id, ego, and super ego," or "the child within," or "subconscious" versus "inner-conscious," we believe the value is measured by how well you feel in the end. The same applies here. Any structure is arbitrary. Our application with more than seven thousand clients has shown dramatic results. If next week, a system with yet another paradigm shift helps more people find their inner peace, be assured we will shift systems. So dive in. Test the waters. Find your insights and do what works for you. Let the adventure begin.

Four Faces of
Let Go & Live

(*Birthplace of* NO BAD FEELINGS!)

Face 1: June

As a little girl I was painfully shy. Considering the later emergence of my "Sherman tank" personality, this may be hard for my friends to believe. I'm sure they have no idea how difficult it was for me to be at ease with youngsters my own age. Grownups presented no problem. They didn't expect much from a small child. My chums, however, were a different story. I never felt quite good enough when I was with them. I wasn't up to their expected, indeterminate standard. (Whether I really was or not, I've conveniently forgotten.) As much as I loved the nuns, their "human sinner" scenario didn't help a bit. Although they emphasized my only hope for rescue was the Almighty, I was equally certain my worldly salvation lay in how much I accomplished. Hence, my drive to feel good enough and avoid everything that was not good enough, raised my banner of duality to its heights.

Feeling lonely and separate, I never noticed how many of my peers were going through exactly the same process. It wasn't until over half a century later that I realized standards, mine and everyone else's, are not universal. What works for one is totally useless for another, and even the most rigid standards are subject to constant change.

By the time I was fifteen, I'd investigated many formal religions and participated in quite a few. I had come to one odd conclusion—at least for a teenager. Feelings were not worthy things, since they were seldom if ever mentioned in holy books. Love and anger were the two exceptions. Love was a duty you owed to others, but *you* had to earn it, which was very confusing. Anger was allowed only by God. Feelings were not something to be respected. They were seldom, if ever, discussed. We were simply told what we were to feel. Outside of that, feelings were an amorphous process that was best left unnoticed—except maybe with your mother, your doctor, or your best friend—something like menstruation or bathroom habits.

The Taoist philosophy seemed to have respect for all things, but in 1940, there wasn't a lot of material around on the subject. With World War II just around the corner, "respect for all things" was hardly the order of the day. Some people claim "feelings ran high in those days." That's not true. I was there. *Resistance* to feelings ran high, which is quite different.

It was about that time I made a choice. I decided to let go of my commitment to save the world from being not good enough, being below standard, and devote my time and energy to finding out about feelings. I'd go some place where feelings were not only respected, but cherished. Welcome to the theater, Miss Graham!

From that time to the present, feelings and emotions have been of paramount concern. It has seemed to me, if we want to know who we are, what we're doing, and why, we have to take a good look at what we are feeling. Investigating feelings has been a good part of my life. Not all my life. I've been married several times. I've been blessed with two wonderful children and four fantastic grandchildren. I must admit that up until recently, I wasn't a very good wife. I wasn't the best of mothers either. If I had it to do over, of course, I'd behave quite differently. But then, wouldn't we all? I have a strong hunch I wouldn't make the same mistakes only because I'd be too busy making new ones.

My background leading up to *No Bad Feelings!* is as diversified as it could possibly be, considering the main commitment was supposedly about feelings. I was a member of a small group in Great Falls, Montana, which I believe was one of the first to introduce psycho-drama. It was from these sessions a process was devised and tried out in the Actor's Studio many years later. I worked in the theater at the University of Iowa. I did summer stock and little theater, including a show David Merrick directed. He suggested to my parents that I come to New York to do the part. They would have none of it. I was to have a simple, normal, Midwestern life.

One marriage, one divorce, and two children later, I arrived in New York with ninety-nine dollars in the bank and the whole world in which to make a living. I guess I never behaved in a manner my St. Louis family considered normal. I have since recognized that although I may not be considered "normal," I am very ordinary, at least as far as feelings are concerned.

Thanks to Betty Furness, the legendary commercial spokeswoman, I landed a contract with *Westinghouse Studio One* a month after my arrival. As if this weren't fortune enough, one night in February 1954, I began my three minute commercial with a huge platter of turkey in my hands. The plan was to open the door with my elbow. The commercial was titled "Look Ma No Hands." However, since the door worked electronically, and someone had kicked the plug out just prior to the commercial break, my efforts were in vain. I managed to use my passion for improvisation to keep from fainting on the spot, and my commercial career was made. That blooper is still famous. With film and tape, a mistake like that can't happen these days. They will just reshoot. Back then, you were out there on your own, and whatever happened, whoever was responsible, the final resolution was up to you. It was an amazing lesson in being in the moment and dealing with what was. Although that break provided a great deal of financial security for myself and my family, it did not evoke the greatest feeling of pride to have your fame built on a mistake, especially for someone who has a button about standards.

From that time on, I was never out of work, except during the McCarthy era when I was blackballed from *both* sides—right and left. I think I must rate a special title for that one. Fortunately, it only lasted for four weeks and it turned out to be a case of mistaken identity, but it was a harrowing experience to go through.

After several thousand commercials, where feelings were at least partially limited, the plunge to soap operas was not unexpected. This is one area where feelings were not only respected, but required—every day—five days a week—*live*—with no retakes and no margin for error. For those of you who are used to today's taped and filmed presentations, it's hard to imagine that in the early days of TV, what you saw on your screen was what was happening in the studio at that very moment. If there was a mistake, a crisis, or a catastrophe, that's exactly what the viewer saw. I spent eight years in daytime television and was even nominated for an Emmy, which I lost to Captain Kangaroo. In those days, all daytime television was linked together. Soaps were considered—you've got it—not quite up to standard, or at least not up to the nighttime standards, in the golden age of TV. (Are you beginning to see a pattern here?)

I was able to do nighttime shows, and I did most all of them. In those days, there were only a handful of dramatic shows each week. Most of them emanated from New York City, and it wasn't unusual for an energetic actor to have appeared on every one of them in a reasonably short period of time. I continued to do some commercials. One required me to fly out to

L.A. to do the show *Playhouse 90*, leave Television City, and catch the red eye back to New York in time for the following morning's rehearsal. I also had a few extra moments to do some panel shows with all the Who's Who in television. I even indulged in theater, when the writers of *The Secret Storm* and later *The Guiding Light* would work on a story line in which my character could take some time off.

As you can guess, my schedule didn't leave much room for self-investigation or personal inquiry. I was too busy making a name for myself, the identity of which I hadn't a clue. It wasn't until my daughter suggested I take a class now called "The Silva Method" that I again began to search for who I was, what I was really doing, and how I honestly felt. I was so taken with the class that I became an instructor. This meant I was to give instruction in meditation for ten hours a day, four days in a row. I had finally come home. I turned more of my attention from my feelings on the stage to helping other people get in touch with feelings they had not expressed and hadn't even realized were there. I found this work more rewarding than anything else I had done in my life. I was sure, as are most people who are on the road to self-discovery, I had found *the* answer to life.

But on November 5, 1975, lying on a gurney in Memorial Sloan-Kettering Cancer Center, I realized that I not only didn't have the answer, I wasn't even sure of the question. I was scheduled to be wheeled into surgery to have a mastectomy when a little voice inside my head began reading me the riot act. Without going into details, I was informed, in no uncertain terms, that unless I changed my perception of what life was really about, I might just as well not bother to come out of the anesthesia. Unless I gave more than lip service to discovering what this whole agenda was about, I was going nowhere with nothing. I'd missed the whole point.

Well! That's quite a proclamation for a hotshot TV star who thinks she has all the answers. However, I *did* listen. I *did* take the words to heart, even though I hadn't the slightest idea what to do next.

Four weeks later I went back to work, and I met Jim Spencer, who was to teach me more about feelings and more about life than I honestly wanted to know.

Face 2: Jim

For as long as I can remember, I have been fascinated with "structure." That fascination has taken on many forms. Sometimes it is rebelling against any structure imposed on me by others, and sometimes it is getting so caught up in structure as to become a rigid rule book. It is also a fascination with architecture and the how-to of construction. This how-to approach spilled over into social structures and the human psyche.

Growing up with a Michigan state trooper for a father, we moved around the state a lot. I had the opportunity to live in nine different houses before starting high school. Although the towns were all small, they still showed me the correct social structure was different in each.

What bewildered me the most was the variety of church rules. Although it was always the same denomination of Protestantism, the how-to—or rather the how-not-to—changed from town to town. One place you could see movies, but gambling was a sin. The next place, bingo was part of the church fundraising, but movies were denounced as godless influences. My interest in religious structure fractured the day I was loudly condemned to hell for including dancing as part of the Youth Fellowship Celebration. As I righteously exited the minister's office, I nearly toppled three gossips listening at the keyhole. Somehow I sensed the workings of the universe must be somewhat larger in scope than the politics of that church.

Fortunately, I was inspired by two high school teachers who approached both science and math as great adventures in discovering the how-to of this mechanistic universe. What a prize Mr. York and Mr. Rudd dangled in front of me.

Graduation from high school presented a new dilemma: Which college should I attend? Since I would be paying every penny, the only feasible option was in-state tuition. Thankfully, the University of Michigan had an excellent program in architecture. The very idea of a life spent exploring and creating at a drafting table made me drool with anticipation. However, Michigan State University offered a great program in psychology. Charting the structure of the human psyche and perhaps getting a handle on my own turbulent feelings also held great appeal. Indecision had me in a hammerlock, so I tossed the proverbial coin into the air. Heads, psychology—tails, architecture. When it landed heads up, I filled out my application to MSU and took the first step toward the inexact science of Freud, Jung, Skinner, Adler, and others.

The conflicting, confusing, and often contradictory theories of humanistic psychology versus clinical, versus behavioral, versus Freudian, versus transpersonal, left me in a paradigm of "versus" with no clear structure. This was also the late sixties. Hugh Hefner was rocking the sexually repressed, while Diana Ross and Motown were rocking the dance floor. The social structure of narrow ties and crew cuts was replaced by love beads, long hair (Unchristian? Figure that one out. Have you ever seen a depiction of Jesus with a crew cut?), and tie-dyed everything. My father the state trooper was pro-Nixon and ready to banish all college protestors. (If only Kent State could have been in his area of jurisdiction.) Nixon was upholding his belief structure by sacrificing hundreds of thousands of my fellow students in Vietnam. I was incredibly confused, challenged, and disoriented, learning about surviving through shifting paradigms.

Another paradigm shift that caught me unprepared was the quiet and clear faith of my steady girlfriend, Barbara. While visiting her family in Chicago, I watched her brother break his arm in a soccer match. The devout Christian Science parents rushed over and told him if he was in a state of mind to practice his beliefs, they would get a practitioner and work with him. If, however, he wasn't ready for that, they would have him in the hospital in five minutes. I was blown away by their faith and lack of imposing church practices if he wasn't ready for them. These people manifested miracles and also respected that real faith is a moment-to-moment thing. The son opted for metaphysical healing and by the next morning his arm was 100 percent. Yes, I started studying with a Christian Science practitioner but when it came to the body being only illusion, I just wasn't ready. Going further into Spirit, oneness, and beyond-the-separate-self would have to wait.

College graduation was a real low point. I had done all the required courses and more. I had an expensive degree and what I considered a poverty level education. Disheartened, I sought a job in Grand Rapids with an old-line office furniture company. They only hired college graduates with degrees in business. I was desperate for a job and convinced them a psychologist could handle sales and complaints much better than someone with Accounting 101. Besides, I had taken classes with titles like Love and Aggression and Abnormal Psychology. What is selling but a balance between love and aggression, while dealing with all their abnormal behaviors and concerns?

I got the job, I got the eighty-hour work week, I got the stress, and I got the insight that I was in over my head. But at least I could tour clients through the factory and explain the how-to of transforming raw lumber into an expensive lacquered office suite for top executives. I loved touching the desk and holding something tangible while I explained delivery would only take twenty-six weeks. Some of these elite executives were transferred, retired, or deceased before their furniture was shipped. Come to think of it, I was in Grand Rapids about twenty-six weeks before I was shipped to the New York City office/showroom. I did have twenty-four hours' notice to prepare for the leap to the Big Apple. Convinced I would be mugged on the flight and die of air pollution within the week, I was bowled over by the nighttime skyline of NYC. I was still en route across the Fifty-Ninth Street Bridge when a revelation erupted through me: "I have just come home!"

It was spring 1971 and at age twenty-two, I had a place to sink my roots. My new home was as dysfunctional as the old ones, but the level of excitement and discovery was explosive. Socially, the many structures of New York and the diversity of its ethnic groups was the beginning of a real education. The architectural array was inspiring and never ending. The cosmic humor in all of this was that I had turned down architecture to pursue psychology. Now, I was working with the biggest and best architectural firms in NYC. Had I become an architect, would I have been designing psychology clinics and padded rooms? You just can't leave yourself behind, no matter where you travel.

The next five years were worth a master's degree in psychology. I was living either a double life or a balanced life. By day it was corporate sales, office politics, designer suits, and awkward luncheons with clients who would never become friends. But nighttime was *my* time. Early evening was spent in classes at five different colleges. I was hungry to learn and the opportunities were endless. Nighttime was bomber jackets, blue jeans, Lincoln Center, Broadway, Little Italy, and Greenwich Village. Late night disco rounded out the day. I was in my twenties in the city that doesn't sleep, and I was having it all! That only served to point out that something crucial was missing. But what?

A coworker introduced me to transcendental meditation (TM). Horizons broadened, life took on new depth, and the stress-induced headache I created every day disappeared after twenty minutes of meditation. Wow. Those behavioral psychology professors had never even mentioned meditation. Every day at work I stressed out and every day after work I melted away into Maharishi land before racing off to night school.

My fascination with how-to had developed into a lifestyle of how to keep juggling too many things and make it all look effortless. My brother, whom I had introduced to TM, returned the favor and introduced me to Silva Mind Control. As I would soon discover, Silva was one of the first seminars developed in this country to incorporate meditation techniques with the power of positive thinking and creative visualization. The four-day seminar was geared to creative problem solving, developing intuition, and improving memory. It was the fore-runner of EST (Erhart Seminar Training) and many other offshoot programs. It was so successful it was taught in more than twenty-eight countries around the world.

My brother had just taken the course in Florida and called to tell me it would do wonders for my juggling act. A strange set of circumstances led to my night school class being can-celed on the evening June Graham was giving an introductory lecture for Silva. I hastened to Midtown to catch her sales pitch and decide if it could help my sales pitch. She was bright, ar-ticulate, successful, and beautiful. She explained how the Silva course would help us to incorporate our intuition and live more successful lives with less stress. The whole thing sounded great.

However, there was something about her that set off alarm bells in my head. I was writing out the check and reserving a space in the Valentine's Day class while a voice in my head was screaming, "I don't have the time, I don't have the money. I don't like this woman. Don't do this." I schizophrenically agreed with the voice in my head as I handed the check over and said, "See you soon." If this was the beginning of hearing my intuition, I was going to be in major conflict.

The four-day seminar began and I carefully placed myself near the back of the room, close to the exit door. June had a rapier wit, an encyclopedic memory for research to support her material, and a charm I found appealing and disruptive at the same time. She explained the Silva Method of meditation so clearly and easily I dove into it as a great way to complement TM. I loved the meditations and my heretofore silent intuition sprang into action. During every meditation I was getting clear messages on how to resolve my business problems. What unsettled me was, after only three meditations, I somehow began to hear in my head what June was about to say aloud before she said it. It was like watching a foreign film where the words are not synchronized to the lip movements. I found this new experience both disturbing and reassuring. My paradigms weren't just shifting, they were hitting 8.6 on the Richter scale.

By the end of the second day of the seminar we learned how to "program to have dreams to solve problems." I had never remembered my dreams, except for the occasional nightmare. We had five days to practice before concluding the seminar on the next weekend. Much to my surprise, I began remembering parts of dreams but none of them solved business problems; they seemed to be more about the how-to of levels of consciousness. I appeared back at class early and shared with June my frustration with half-remembered, cosmic-content dreams. As I shared a few memories, she gasped and said, "I had the same dreams! This is how they ended." As she began telling me the endings, the dreams reappeared in living technicolor in my memory before she finished speaking. I thanked her, returned to my seat and waited to hear the theme music from the *Twilight Zone*. It felt like the best thing that had ever happened to me. I think I went comatose for the next meditation. Then, one surprising insight after another unfolded, until the seminar ended. I had just dropped the structure I had called my life and stepped into a new paradigm of exploring consciousness.

Shortly thereafter, I dropped my career and began working with June. By the next fall we were working, living, and loving together. Because of a twenty-four-year age difference and the fact that we were willing to drop the old structure and embrace a new adventure, many of our friends told us we were crazy and disappeared from sight. One dear friend kept us on track when she said, "Darlings, it is obvious you're in love. You have something very special that everyone else wants. Now don't mess that up!"

Face 3: Let Go & Live

We stayed with the Silva Method for a couple of years as team teachers. June published her first book *Pieces*. It was a compilation of short essays and pieces she had written about living, dying, celebrating, and learning to love. It served as a reminder of some of the possibilities that could happen as a result of using the ideas presented in class.

We were blessed with the unique gifts and challenges every student brought to the class. The biggest challenge took the form of a question: "Why is it that by meditating on a specific end result, it will manifest much of the time, but not all of the time?" We had been teaching the power of positive thinking at a meditative level and witnessed numerous "miracles," especially regarding health issues. So why didn't it work consistently? That question led us on a quest to every workshop, class, and lecture we could find. While we enjoyed hundreds of classes, we didn't find any clear answers. After five years of intensive study of world religions, we were ordained as interfaith ministers at the Communion of Souls Seminary. Even this scope of study didn't fully answer our questions. Some clues came from the Kabbalah, and some from scraps of the original Christian text, written before the Council of Nicea in 325 A.D. Some of the most helpful clues came from the nondualistic traditions such as Buddhism. Dualism carries the judgment that if one thing is good then its polarity must be bad. Nondualism is more inclusive. It respects the importance of imperfection as well as perfection; sadness as well as joy.

As for seminars, "The Sedona Method," created by physicist Lester Levinson, was the closest thing we found to a true nondualistic principle. By this time, we were so busy with the great search for answers out there, we weren't being quiet enough to see what was right under our noses. Then, one night, our dreams began unfolding a paradigm of oneness, respect for all things, and unconditional acceptance. Easier said than lived, but we began putting it into our daily practice, step by step.

A new how-to for experiencing feelings as part of a nondualistic paradigm began to emerge. As we discussed our fledgling steps, a friend insisted we share them. "The best way to learn something," she reminded us, "is to teach it." Two weeks later, seventy-eight people arrived at our premiere seminar and Let Go & Live was off to a clumsy start. Shortly thereafter, we incorporated the Let Go & Live Institute as a nonprofit, educational organization. We waved goodbye to Silva and let the universe set our course.

The events that followed were anything but uneventful. In the seventies, self-help books crowded the shelves, and seminars blossomed like dandelions in a spring rain. "Positive thinking" was the buzz phrase of the "New Age." Whenever the question was raised about why these spectacular processes didn't work *every* time, the company answer was always that the practitioner wasn't following the process correctly.

When Let Go & Live premiered in 1979, going beyond dualistic reasoning, seeing polarities as two parts of the same thing rather than either good or bad, was a virtually unheard-of approach in American culture. The accepted practice had always been to go after what was good, eliminate what was bad, and the twain were never to meet. Suggesting that trying to destroy what we considered bad was far from thinking positively, came as quite a shock. However, as more people questioned their goals and their desired end results, they discovered Let Go & Live's principle really worked, especially in the world of feelings.

The principle of going for a feeling you wanted, rather than trying to avoid one you didn't want was a huge change of perception and an enormous challenge for many. It was almost ten years before most people had begun to alter their paradigms. However, bit by bit, we began receiving comments about the course like the following:

- Let Go & Live was a release from pain that I truly had felt was impossible. (G. F. Bruyette, Bloomfield, Connecticut)

- Thank you for giving me back my life. (Wanette Baylo, New York, New York)

- After sixteen years with a knot in my stomach, a knot of all the feelings I couldn't express, I've finally had a week with no knots. (Jerry Kilgore, Wimberly, Texas)

- I've never received so much as I did from Let Go & Live. (Lisa Bhavsar, Lexington, Kentucky)

- You gave me tools to see myself. (Suzy Pruden, Beverly Hills, California)

- Since I was a child, I've kept my feelings inside myself. Now it's like opening a door that's been locked for many years. A door to a new way of life—a door to a clean, drug-free life, a door to life itself. (Paul, New York, New York)

- Let Go & Live is an inspiration. (Allesyn Charles, Ala Wai School, Honolulu, Hawaii)

- It's about time someone said it's okay to feel. (Carolyn Maynard, Cherry Hill, New Jersey)

- The most exciting cancer therapy I've heard yet. (Betsy Meyers, RN, Reach to Recovery, American Cancer Society, New York, New York)

- It was the greatest experience of my life. I've never experienced life so fully. (Allen Somar, Poughkeepsie, New York)

- This has opened up my eyes to the real me that I've been running away from. (Jessie Erlanger, Forest Hills, New York)

- I wish your work could be included as part of the curriculum in all colleges and universities. (Dr. A. Raman, Assawiya, Libya)
- My God. It really works! (Bill Slack, New York, New York)

Although the material in Let Go & Live has evolved over the years, the main theme has remained constant. The theme is letting go of the resistance to feelings. The majority of our seminars have been open to a wide mix of individuals. However, we have also worked with specialized groups, each with its own particular focus.

We presented one seminar in a cloistered nunnery in the Bronx. The nuns there keep "perpetual adoration." That means there is around-the-clock prayer at the altar, and each nun has an hour-long shift. The problem we addressed was the inner fight with "uncharitable feelings." Many of the nuns confessed that the first half hour of prayer was filled with mental chatter, such as, "I know Sister Rose Eva has arthritis, but I'm tired of always covering her kitchen duties as she moans about her arthritis flaring up." The sisters wanted help in clearing their minds and hearts so they could get to the state of deep prayer quicker. Letting go of the inner fight with feeling resentful provided just what they needed.

The Vietnam Veterans Council asked us to tailor a workshop to their needs. Clarifying their specific "resistances" wasn't easy for them, but during the course, the key issues surfaced. Going through hell to come home a hero is one thing. Coming home and being perceived as a fool or a crazed killer of villagers triggered deep feelings of invalidation for them. This was their major issue and their major resistance.

Through this work, we met and worked with the Vietnam Veterans Theater Group in Manhattan. Here, we were able to use June's theater background in a new light. Theater presents a superb opportunity to recognize and explore how we're really relating to feelings.

About this time we published our book *Beyond the Words*, a guide to communication skills. It offered sixteen techniques for communicating feelings so that a true communion could happen beyond the words alone. We presented "Communication/Communion" workshops using theater techniques to help people see where they were blocking their feelings. For example, a number of students "couldn't ask the boss for a raise," for fear of being rejected. After the workshop they were able to move through that fear. The biggest breakthrough had to do with couples being able to honestly and freely communicate affection, concern, and even disagreement.

Our next specialty group for Let Go & Live was the America Cancer Society. We worked with six hundred mastectomy patients through Reach to Recovery. June's mastectomy experience and the fact that we had begun our relationship after the surgery gave us an immediate connection. Feelings that had been carefully locked away for years were ready to surface for most of the women in the recovery period following surgery.

Shortly after our experience with the Cancer Society we were contacted by the NYC Gay Men's Health Crisis. The AIDS epidemic was underway. The disease was horrific and many of the early treatments were even worse. However, out of such ugliness and after much work on freeing the feelings and healing the spirit, all but one of the patients we worked with said, "AIDS may have been the best thing that ever happened to me." This alone made both the group and individual work the most challenging and the most rewarding we'd ever experienced.

Our next round of custom seminars involved corporations. "Empowered Team Building" was catching on in business, but often it failed to address feelings. How do you empower someone filled with either self-doubt or lack of trust? How do you build a team with people too angry or too fearful to confide and cooperate? Addressing these feelings seemed to be the obvious answer.

We had the opportunity to work with a major insurance company, the Chase Bank, DisneyWorld, and others. Our success depended totally on how willing management was to allow personal empowerment in the organization. We had several hits and one error.

Thinking back on our corporate work, we must not forget our seminar for the United Nations. While the individuals enjoyed it, we don't begin to assume we made even a dent in the giant commitment to "political protective protocol." Hopefully, the inner peace that comes from respecting one another's feelings will one day allow the UN to be a leading force in world peace. Who can tell?

Our occasional corporate adventures spurred the creation of our book *A Dictionary for New Age Drop-Outs*. It used a dictionary format to present sometimes serious and sometimes humorous insights into the human condition. The French translation was a delight for us. Instead of dictionary, it was translated as "reflectionary," ideas on which one can reflect.

In 1988 an editor from Ballantine Books took our seminar. She asked us to show her any writings on the course material, and in 1989 *Let Go & Live* was published. The first printing of thirteen thousand copies sold out, and we were able to reach a wider audience. We had never advertised our seminars, but the word of mouth had spread far and wide. It wasn't long before we were doing not only seminars but private counseling as well. Some of the sessions were at our house; others, with clients from Africa and Australia, were conducted over the phone.

As early as 1985, we had more clients than the two of us could handle, so we had started teacher training. Our original list of seventy-eight students had grown to seven or eight thousand. Every day and night was filled with classes, counseling, or teacher training. At one point, we had thirteen weeks with only one brief evening to ourselves. We joyously planned get-togethers in the summer, Oktoberfest retreats in the fall, celebrations in the winter, and by spring, we were usually in bed with colds.

In the summer of 1992, we decided to take some time off. We had again gotten so involved with "out there," that we had neglected "in here," and it was crying for attention. So, in August 1992, we moved to a tiny town in Colorado, where we occasionally offer seminars. Since we are listed in the Salida, Colorado, phone book, it is easy to continue with our telephone counseling nationwide. There are still four fully trained instructors in the New York area doing their own form of Let Go & Live, some through counseling, others through seminars and meditation classes.

While we are spending less time teaching Let Go & Live, we're spending more time living it, and that's even more fun. We keep experiencing astounding things, some of which we're passing on to you. We're watching our feelings ebb and flow, arrive and move on. We've finally allowed them to be free to do so. We're free too because we've made friends with every one of them.

Face 4: You, the Reader

This is a face we don't know—yet. However, from the clients who have shared their feelings with us and the readers who have shared their feedback about our books, we have a rough profile. Whether working with drug addicts, nuns, or CEOs, the common denominator is feelings. We relate to them in very individual ways but the feelings are always the same.

The contribution of our book is, we hope, the understanding and acceptance of feelings. Not just the ones we like but the ones we don't like, and the ones we don't really know. If we are to pursue the study of self-discovery, part of the discovery must necessarily include feelings. Knowing and owning our feelings is as important as knowing and owning our bodies. Our emotional well-being is as important as our physical. Often the latter depends on the former. We're all one big conglomerate. Each part of us is in some way a part of all the others, and we are all a part of one another.

It's hoped that the journey of exploring our feelings will be not only an inspiring one, but a freeing one as well. Who knows? Some of these feelings we've avoided and kept in dry ice may be just the ones that hold the key to the happiness we've been longing for all along.

We know from experience that some of you will be skeptical and some of you won't. Some of you will say this book has changed your life. Some of you won't even finish it. One thing you will all do, whether you want to or not, is *feel*. That's what we human beings do best. So until we meet some day—if we meet some day—thank you for letting us share with you.

After each chapter is a tiny verse with seventeen syllables, which is the form of haiku. These are not strictly haiku but contain a simple idea about each chapter. We call them "fortune cookies."

✦ ✦ ✦

Our joy is finding
that nothing is separate, and
that we are all one.

No Bad Feelings!
PART I

CHAPTER 1

In Defense of Feelings

This is a book about discovering feelings, accepting and appreciating feelings, and using them for a fuller, more joyful life.

"What," you may ask, "do you mean by feelings?" We all have very different ideas of what feelings mean to us. What does someone mean by "You hurt my feelings?" Which of her feelings suffered from the blow? Surely, not the same ones as, "I have a feeling it's going to rain" or "I don't know how I feel about this new merger." All of these are feelings to be sure.

The feelings that *we* will be talking about in this book will include the above and hundreds more. So let's start at the beginning with the history of feelings.

The History of Feelings

About thirty thousand years ago, when we humans had just learned to walk on two feet, our behavior, as well as our appearance, was quite different. Our decisions could not have been considered rational ones, since our minds were not concerned with a myriad of facts and figures from which we could choose.

We depended entirely on our intuitive talents, which pre-sented themselves as feelings. Homo erectus, being unfamiliar with time zones and temperature levels, would never be heard to say, "According to the almanac, we'd better head south be-fore the first anticipated snow, the last week in October." He would more likely have motioned to his family, and later his tribe, as the result of a feeling he had. Most of the time he was pretty accurate. How do we know? If not, the human race would have died out.

This mode of intuitive reasoning, or feeling behavior, con-tinued uninterrupted through the nomadic hunter-gatherer age. All those years we depended entirely on our intuition for our food, living space, movement, social hierarchy, and so forth. Then, with the birth of the Agrarian Age, more knowledge be-came based on information and less on intuition and feelings. By the turn of the nineteenth century, feelings were no longer respected and revered but looked down on and denied. At the height of the Victorian era, feelings were repressed and hid-den whenever possible. Intuition disappeared in favor of the newly discovered information. Only a few isolated philoso-phers and authors kept feelings alive, albeit the feelings were mostly concerned with unrequited love.

Today, we have progressed far enough to see that a bal-anced life requires more than just rational thinking *or* intuitive thinking. It calls for a combination of both. We are relearning the value of feelings and the importance of intuition. Feelings are no longer stepchildren, and we are beginning to realize that it's feelings *along* with information that makes us human. While our actions may be the result of considered informa-tion, if the consequence involves a feeling that we want desperately to avoid, we can be certain that it will be a decid-ing factor. Feelings are the weather vanes, the navigators of our behavior.

What Is A Feeling?

Whether we like it or not, *all human behavior is built on feelings.*

✦ ✦ ✦

Reminder: Here is the first "paradigm shift." Whether you currently agree with this or not, read on as though it were true. This will allow a more empowered perspective, which can augment what you already see.

✦ ✦ ✦

All human behavior is built on feelings. It may not be a feeling of which we are aware or even recognize. We are not speaking of a physical sensation. That *always* gets our attention. We're referring to what Merriam-Webster calls "susceptibility to impression; quality of one's awareness, reasoned opinion, or capacity to respond emotionally."

As you can see, the experts don't make the definition of feelings any easier to pinpoint. The best explanation of the feelings to which we'll be referring is, "How we relate emotionally to what is happening." For example, when given a compliment, some people are elated because they feel important and like that feeling. Others are embarrassed because when attention is brought to them, they feel insecure and don't like that feeling.

There are levels and levels of feelings. Remember the 2000 Olympics, when the Russian gymnasts pulled off their silver medals? They were obviously upset because underneath, they felt invalidated, not good enough, below standard, or something of the sort. Compare their behavior to those who received the bronze medal with excitement and elation. Their feelings about getting a lesser medal were obviously nothing like the Russians'. Each related emotionally to the situation in his or her own way. Some of the athletes, while relating emotionally, didn't show their feelings, yet others did. However, all of the athletes, you can be sure, had their own feelings.

When we say, "I feel happy," it's because the feeling underneath is powerful, productive, successful, worthy, abundant, special, or some other feeling we enjoy. If we're unhappy, it's probably the result of feeling powerless, unproductive, unsuccessful, unworthy, empty, ordinary, or some other feeling we don't like. These are the feelings we'll be talking about. They're the ones we're going to learn to identify, investigate, and use to live a fuller, more joyful, more aware life. We're not asking you to agree with our philosophy, we're just asking you to try the process and see if you don't *feel* better.

How We Use Feelings

When we said all human behavior is built on feelings, we meant that every choice we make is based on a feeling we want to experience or want to avoid experiencing. The clothes we choose to wear, the food we decide to eat, and the career we select to follow are all built on feelings.

Some people choose clothes that make them stand out in a crowd. Perhaps they want to feel unique or special. Others choose outfits that blend into their surroundings. They enjoy a feeling of security and a sense of belonging. Others will say, "There was no feeling. I wore it because it was the only thing clean and pressed." Further examination will show that to stop and press something else would have brought up a feeling of drudgery or missing out or purposelessness. Wearing it was about avoiding those feelings and getting on to others we like better.

Choosing a mate to share a feeling of discovery is an obvious example of wanting to experience a feeling. Settling for a mate because we're afraid he or she might be our last chance, and we'll end up feeling lonely, is an example of trying to avoid a feeling. The big surprise is that we're going to meet the feeling anyway. (More on that later.)

We may not be aware of *what* we are feeling and what feeling is causing us to make our particular choice, but rest assured,

Ingles

1. dinner for tonite
2. ½ + ½
3. milk

there is always a feeling there. No matter how strong an intuitive hunch, or how well thought-out a rational idea may be, if underneath we might have to face a feeling that we don't like, we won't pursue either one.

Since our feelings are the impetus for our choice of behavior, we might reflect on the fact that in the United States every few seconds someone is robbed. Every few minutes someone is beaten, stabbed, raped, or murdered. Every few days a youngster kills his or her parents. There are more than twenty million alcoholics and drug addicts. Suicide has increased almost 100 percent, especially with teenagers. We don't have to be princes or princesses of pessimism to recognize that this frighteningly increasing pattern warrants a closer look at the feelings behind such behavior.

It is generally conceded that everything we see is colored by our perceptions, which in turn are influenced, to a large extent, by our feelings. Consequently, everything we see, mirrors to some degree what we are feeling. If we are feeling expansive, the world we perceive will be expansive. If we are feeling confined, everything within our periphery will reflect confinement.

Feelings Have Had Bad Press

As we mentioned, over the past few generations, we have become a society that doesn't cherish our feelings. We not only deny them, we even reward ourselves for how well we can hide them. Today, we are given all manner of prescriptions, not only to cover up the feelings we don't like, but also the ones we do. Expressing our feelings has become downright unprofessional and unacceptable. A nonfeeler's idea of a perfect existence today is where he or she is never challenged, afraid, angry, or upset in any way. It's an interesting fantasy, but it is just that—a fantasy.

Why do we play this purposeless game of denial? Most of us have been told over and over that acknowledging and experiencing feelings is immature and unacceptable. Old cliches like, "Big girls don't cry, and boys don't cry at all," are all too familiar. Consequently, we see our feelings as things we were born with but no longer need—like our appendix. If, in some unguarded moment, we *do* manage to feel something, we certainly don't let it be known. As a result, most of us have buried our feelings, poured concrete over them, and put up a mall of sophisticated superficiality. We've become experts at charming, gracious, uninvolved behavior. While we may deny our feelings, we actually crave experiencing them somewhere we believe will be safe.

To see how much we desire to feel, let's take a look at the most popular movies. Something like 40 percent are made with the sole purpose of scaring the "yell" out of us in a darkened theater where no one can see us. While you personally may not go to scary movies, millions of people do. Hordes flock to theaters across the country to see terrified victims stalked, clubbed, clawed, smothered, stabbed, butchered, and anything else that can elicit an honest feeling. In some cases it is feeling powerless, other times it is feeling exhilarated.

Often, the feelings sought are ones we don't allow in our daily life. It is somehow acceptable to get excited in a sporting event but taboo to express the same feeling somewhere else. We have all observed people who get absolutely apoplectic at a baseball game, but are incapable of getting excited about anything their spouse or children do.

A multitude of songs are written for the express purpose of eliciting feelings. Country music provides some of the best examples. Disappointment, betrayal, and abandonment are just a few of the bittersweet sensations we enjoy while listening to our favorite musical performers.

Over half of the present book market is dedicated to romance novels. These books are hardly purchased for acquiring information. They create a safe fantasy world where our passions are reciprocated and our longings are fulfilled rather than denied.

More and more medical and psychology circles are recognizing that human behavior is built on feelings. Many doctors agree that "tears that have no outlet can cause the body to weep." Blocking our feelings can not only depress us, but cause corresponding blockages in the body. Specific examples will be discussed in Chapter 4. Feelings are an essential part of our very nature.

Nearly everything we do is built on feelings. Our very priorities are the result of how we want or don't want to feel. We may want a big house to feel up to standard or not feel below standard. We want to be in control so we can feel important or not feel unimportant. We want to be famous so we can feel validated, or we choose the shadows rather than the limelight, to avoid the possibility of feeling foolish and invalidated.

We Remember Feelings

Most memory is built on feelings; thus abstract concepts are harder to learn. For example, we can all remember the first time we fell in love. The most intricate details are etched in our mind along with the feeling. We tend to remember, with amazing clarity, a feeling of validation, or pride, or discovery, while an abstract discussion of philosophy may not be retained for twenty-four hours—even for a final exam. There is little feeling behind abstractions for most of us. We might not be able to remember where we were at noontime three weeks ago, but those of us who are old enough will remember, with absolute recall, where we were around noontime the day John F. Kennedy was shot. Why? Because we had strong *feelings* attached to the incident.

Feelings Are Natural

Sometimes we forget that as humans, we are subject to nature's cycles. We have not only our entrances and exits, as Shakespeare noted, but our expansions and contractions, as well. We breathe in and out without thinking they are two activities. Stop exhaling or inhaling for a few minutes, and you'll get the point. Feelings are no exception. Having ups and downs is not only natural, but essential to our well-being.

✦ ✦ ✦

Reminder: This acceptance of "ups and downs as natural" can rock the foundations of those who currently believe that "up is good and down is terrible." This new idea gives us permission to experience all of life and to keep moving through it. Instead of the emotional paralysis of being "down" and needing antidepressants to bear the feeling, we are exploring the process of embracing ups and downs, which allows us to move through without getting stuck.

✦ ✦ ✦

No matter how wonderful our lives become, we will always experience emotional expansions and contractions. This is not suggesting that emotions are an excuse for any behavior. They are not. Wallowing in a feeling is just as self-defeating as subjugating it. Recognizing it, accepting it, experiencing it, and moving on to the next one, is the formula that seems to leave us with the most fulfillment.

Our life does not depend on what happens but on how we feel about what happens; not on who we are but on how we feel about who we are; not on what we have but on how we feel about what we have; not on what we are doing but on how we feel about what we're doing; not on how others respond to us but on how we feel about how others respond to us.

While being responsible for our feelings is one giant step toward our maturity and freedom, there is one feeling for which we are never responsible—someone else's. Nor are they responsible for ours. Most of us have tried shifting some of the responsibility for our feelings onto someone else. We've made the government responsible for our feeling of nationalism; the doctors for our feeling of well-being; the lawyers for our feelings of right and wrong; and, the police for our feeling of security. Despite the charming lyrics of the Frank Sinatra classic, "You Make Me Feel So Young," no one can make us feel anything or hurt us without our expressed permission.

Also, we cannot feel another's feeling any more than they can feel ours. We can notice and recognize what someone is feeling and have our own feeling in response, but we cannot feel what they are feeling. We may join someone in feeling sad, glad, or anything *we* choose. The choice is always ours.

✦ ✦ ✦

Reminder: A large percentage of us disagree with these statements. However, stop and ask yourself, "How would my life be different if I considered this to be true?" Instead of trying to manipulate others into or out of an experience, we could just love them and support them through it. Instead of being manipulated by statements like, "You hurt my feelings," "You ruined my holiday," or "You'll pay for this," we could be open and loving to the person in pain and blame. Isn't that what we both ultimately want?

✦ ✦ ✦

*It takes great courage
to be responsible for
our own emotions.*

CHAPTER 2

All Feelings Come in Pairs
(With a Few Exceptions)

Most of us agree there are two sides to every story and most things in life come in pairs. There would be no back without front, no hot without cold, light without dark. It has often been said that our true happiness lies in knowing the secret of the unity of opposites. This certainly applies to feelings. The instant we create a feeling, we have created its twin. Perhaps, thinking of them as polarities rather than opposites might be of inestimable help, because they are not two different things, but two sides of the same coin, the inhale and the exhale, the yin and the yang. They cannot exist without each other. One automatically defines its twin.

✦ ✦ ✦

Reminder: Most of us act as though these feeling twins were really opposite ends of the spectrum. We strive toward one (freedom), believing that will ensure we will never have to experience the other (confined). Then, we hit confined and either give up in despair or fight harder to have our freedom. Think back to "ups and downs are natural." Freedom and confined are

natural feelings. The more graciously we embrace
confined, the more freedom we experience as well.

✦ ✦ ✦

The following is a list of two dozen of some of the most popular feelings. It is also a list of some of the most unpopular, since the desire to experience one of the partners is usually coupled with a desire to avoid the other.

We feel...

Abundant ... lacking
Adequate ... inadequate
Appreciated ... unappreciated
Complete ... incomplete
Connected ... disconnected
Independent ... dependent
Free ... confined
Full ... empty
Good enough ... not good enough
Important ... unimportant
Included ... excluded
Patient ... impatient
Productive ... unproductive
Purposeful ... purposeless
Responsible ... irresponsible
Secure ... insecure
Special ... ordinary
Successful ... unsuccessful
Superior ... inferior
Understood ... misunderstood
Used ... unused
Validated ... invalidated
Wanted ... unwanted
Worthy ... unworthy

Because feelings come in pairs, they complement each other—as long as we are willing to experience both. *Up* and *down* are complementary experiences. Example: Stand *up* on your tiptoes, lock your knees, and try to jump further *up*. You can't do it. However, once you relax your knees and are willing to bend *down*, you will be able to jump *up*. Of course, you will have to come *down* again.

The same is true with feelings. *In order to experience one, we must be willing to experience the other.* We cannot feel free without having experienced limitation. Once we refuse to accept a feeling, we have automatically cast out its twin. Being unaware of your feelings is like driving a car with no steering wheel. Not accepting one half of the twin pair is like driving a car with brakes and no accelerator.

Since feelings are an integral part of us, when we're rejecting a feeling, we are also rejecting a part of ourselves. Hence, by refusing to be a whole person, we are limiting ourselves to being less than who we really are.

We need to understand this process; otherwise we strive for one polarity while trying to avoid the other. This practice is called "dualism" and is thought by many to be one of the greatest misinterpretations of life. There are an astonishing number of people who believe a truly successful life consists of being able to avoid all the things you don't like. That would be possible only if we were to lock all darkness away in a drawer so we could experience only light.

Nowhere is this misunderstanding more obvious than in the arena of feelings. The idea that we must always feel full and never empty, always adequate and never inadequate, always included and never excluded is not only contrary to nature but is the cause of a great deal of unhappiness.

What We Resist Persists

Just as feelings come in pairs, so does what we do with them. We can accept or fight them. That's all. We can deny or ignore them, which is just another way of fighting them, but we can't destroy or make them go away, as much as we would like to. We seldom, if ever, feel successful without having experienced the sense of failure first. "If at first you don't succeed," might well be followed by, "fail, fail again."

Still, most of us spend a great part of our lives trying to avoid the half of a feeling pair that we don't like. We then wonder why the other half is so elusive, while the half we're resisting follows us everywhere. Those of us who have an aversion to being controlled will testify to the fact that we meet control freaks everywhere. Some of us can also remember that in school, when we were fighting inadequacy, the only times we could be certain of being called on were when we hadn't finished our assignment. In other words, "What we resist, almost always persists." And yet, we persist in resisting. Our determination is legendary.

There will, of course, be times of confusion. At these times it's best to remember that we can have any feeling we want, as long as we're willing to accept its twin. We can all have the feeling of success, as long as we're willing to experience a failure or two along the way. We'll truly know how it feels to be special when we've also known how ordinary feels. Only when we disconnect from one thing are we free to connect with another.

Of course, if we want to fight feeling foolish, we'll be plagued with "hoof-in-mouth disease." We've all had the experience of wanting to avoid feeling foolish, which is the *one* time we seem to open our mouths only to change feet. We commit to fighting a feeling and consequently lead ourselves to a situation where we can easily have that fight. The most amusing part of the scenario is that when we are faced with an unpleasant situation, we wonder how it could have happened and deny having any part in it. That's probably because it's our nature to seek pleasure and avoid pain. (Running to the angels or from the goblins.) Why? Because, when it comes to feelings, we forget where the pain is coming from. When we're fighting a feeling and we're in pain, we blame the feeling. We conveniently forget that no feeling is hurtful. It is our fight with it that causes our pain. *There are no bad feelings.* No feeling will hurt us. Our aversion to it, on the other hand, can cause unspeakable pain. Conversely, there are no good feelings. Our celebration of them can cause unspeakable pleasure.

✦ ✦ ✦

Reminder: This may seem to contradict everything we have ever experienced. We try to get rid of painful feelings, not realizing that the "trying to get rid of" is the cause of the pain. Embrace the possibilities of this "paradigm shift" and your whole world can open to greater joy and peace. Our approach to the feeling causes our pain or joy. And we can change our approach. That is powerful!

✦ ✦ ✦

Yes, all feelings are basically benevolent. It's the fight that hurts. We will all feel misunderstood, excluded, and unimportant some of the time. Once we know that these feelings are all part of the human experience, we can accept them, learn from them and begin to enjoy them. This approach will help our lives be easier, happier, and a lot more amusing.

(Please note that the following words—fight, resist, avoid, reject, aversion, resistance, and dislike—are all used interchangeably when dealing with feelings. True, they do have different nuances. However, since much of the philosophy in this book is about aversion, denial, and so forth, the same word repeated over and over would become tiresome. Besides, we all resonate to different meanings, and a word that might be meaningful to one person, might be distasteful to another.)

More Resistance

Our fight with or resistance to feelings is a losing battle from the start. When we tell ourselves that we refuse to experience a feeling, we have just paged it on the universal loud speaker. Try closing your eyes and telling yourself, "I will not think of a monkey," and every goblin in the neighborhood will put on a monkey suit. The reason is that there is no mental picture for "not," "no," or "never."

If you don't like speaking in public, which is true of most of us, try standing at a podium with an audience of hundreds and keep telling yourself, "I will not be nervous. I will not be nervous. I will not be nervous," and see what happens. The harder we try to avoid nervousness, the more nervous we feel. The more we deny any feeling, the stronger the battle lines are drawn. Our decision to do battle, or to enjoy, is our commitment. It is to *this* commitment we dedicate each moment of our lives.

Splat!

Several years ago there was a Jules Feiffer cartoon about a woman who came to visit a very wise guru. She asked him how she could reach enlightenment. He closed his eyes for a few moments, then lifted his arm and pointed in a specific direction. The woman took off as indicated, and a short while later a loud *splat* was heard. The woman returned quite confused, again asking for the direction of wisdom and awareness. Again, the guru lifted his arm and pointed in the same direction. Again, the woman followed his lead and again a *splat* was heard, even louder than before. This time the woman returned quite distraught, pleading for directions to true consciousness. The same scenario was repeated, only this time the *splat* was almost deafening. When the woman returned for the third time, she was almost speechless and could only utter, "Where? Which way?" The guru smiled, bowed his head, pointed in the same direction and replied, "That way. One step beyond *splat*."

Mind and Body Are Not Separate

We all hit *splat* with our feelings now and then. Our problem is that often we don't want to go beyond it, until we recognize *splat* is not a punishment, merely a signpost. When we're looking for completeness, consciousness, awareness, and joy, we have to go one step beyond our self-created boundary of nonacceptance. The view from the other side is what we've been looking for. Once we understand that the emotional system is a moving, organic system, just like other systems in our bodies, we will recognize that fighting feelings prolongs them rather than destroys them. Accepting a feeling is the only way to go one step beyond *splat*. *Splat* is the result of our resistance. Acceptance is the only thing that will dissolve it.

Fighting a feeling leads to emotional discomfort, our body experiences physical discomfort as well. Feelings and the emotional system are as important to our bodies as our circulatory or digestive system. If any system is not functioning smoothly, the whole body suffers. If our stomach is rejecting something, or a part of it is missing, we won't be able to digest our food properly. If an artery is clogged and not allowing normal blood flow, we're in deep trouble. The same process applies to the emotional system. Feelings are like cards on a Rolodex. For the most effective use, they must be able to flip easily. If one card is not readily accessible, they all get stuck. If we refuse to accept one feeling, this resistance jams the Rolodex and clogs the system. Just as the malfunction of the respiratory system can cause shortness of breath, and the clogging of the bloodstream can cause heart disorder, so the malfunction of the emotional system can cause stress, pain, unhappiness, and severe illness.

Besides the physical symptoms correlated with our commitment to fight or accept a feeling, there are emotional symptoms as well. These can act as signposts.

✦ ✦ ✦

The symptoms of fighting are pain,
fatigue, and confusion.
The symptoms of acceptance are clarity,
abundance, and freedom.

✦ ✦ ✦

Acceptance Versus Apathy

Knowing that fighting and resisting are painful, we are still often reluctant to accept. We've been told that it's strong to fight and weak not to. Acceptance is not weak but a truly heroic gesture. One act of acceptance and letting go may take more courage than a lifetime of fighting, resisting, and holding on. Acceptance is not apathy. Apathy, like stoicism, is the brittle shell that houses socially acceptable resignation.

Apathy is akin to one of the most sinister four letter words in the English language: *cope.* Coping means forcing ourselves to do something that we really don't want to do and then having to pretend we enjoy it. Coping is a form of resignation, which is really passive resistance. To say, "I'll do it, but I won't like it," doesn't make the task any easier. Coping is an invalidation of the human spirit and one of the greatest causes of the deterioration of the human body. If we have to bottle up our feelings, keep them from the natural flow, how are we affecting our minds, bodies, and spirit? Still, coping is a widely suggested blanket cure-all for an ailing society.

✦ ✦ ✦

Reminder: Coping is often the best choice the old
paradigm can offer, and is a valid step. However, in
this new paradigm, there are options available that

can take us so far beyond coping that it would seem to be a poor choice at best.

✦ ✦ ✦

This is not suggesting we won't have to do things that we don't like. But doing what we don't like—feeling some form of discomfort and pretending that everything is fine—is destructive to the mind and the body. It almost always produces resentment, which will cause further aversion and fight, and sometimes even revenge, which never grows anything worth saving.

To be complete human beings, all people need to feel. Feeling is the strongest bond we all have in common. Experiencing feelings is how we know we're alive and is one of the reasons we *are* alive. If we aren't feeling, we may be existing in our bodies but we aren't truly living.

Acceptance is an energetic, exciting, invigorating practice. Some shining examples of acceptance and the wisdom of going with what's happening rather than fighting against it are steering into a skid, turning a bicycle in the direction we're falling, and the judo method of controlling an attack by swinging our body with the motion coming at us. All these and many more are situations that are improved by accepting rather than resisting, and are actions we sometimes do automatically.

The following is a true story as well as a splendid example of moving from resistance to acceptance.

Harold had a commitment to struggling against disappointment. As a result, disappointment had been hanging around, on and off, for many years. He had battled disappointment through his four years of college. By the time he was twenty-seven, he was somewhat of an expert in this field. It was not easy for him to change his pattern. One day, he was lying on the sofa in his lovely home, triumphantly saying to himself, "I'm in the place I love, with the woman I love, doing just what I love," when a familiar little voice said, "And you're still disappointed, aren't you?" This time, instead of fighting the feeling, as he'd spent years doing, he tried a new commitment.

"Okay," he said, "let's be disappointed. Let's really get into it." In no more than ten minutes, much to his amazement, the disappointment lifted. Once it was accepted, and not for the purpose of eliminating it, the disappointment was content to move on and make room for the next experience. Harold, of course, has met with disappointment since. But, it always comes for a very short visit, almost like an old friend, and hasn't taken up permanent residence, as it had before. And all he did was change his commitment!

✦ ✦ ✦

To solve a riddle,
we might try looking at it
from the other side.

✦ ✦ ✦

CHAPTER 3

There's Nothing Out There
(Or If I Had a Million Dollars I'd Feel Great)

It's not unusual to hear people ask, "How could I *not* be happy in this situation?" Well, the answer is, "Easily." We also hear, "Who could be happy in *that* situation?" The answer to which is, "Anybody who realizes that the situation isn't causing the feeling."

Of all the concepts, all the philosophy suggested in this book, probably the most difficult to accept is that *situations do not cause feelings.*

✦ ✦ ✦

Reminder: Even if you don't agree, go through this chapter and see how you can stop being a victim of circumstance by becoming responsible for your feelings. It won't be easy, because all of our lives we have been told that the reason we feel the way we do is because of what has taken place. The situation has always been held responsible for our feelings. It's no wonder that we seldom, if ever, hear anyone honestly admit, "I did it because I felt like it. No one made me do it. No one coerced me into doing it. I just did it."

✦ ✦ ✦

Of course, situations may expedite or exacerbate feelings, but they don't create them. They are only symbols of our feelings. Were this not so, people in similar situations would experience similar feeling patterns, and they often don't. Four friends sit through the same movie and have totally different feeling responses to it. Identical twins from the same gene pool, with the same genetic transference, brought up in the same surroundings, quite often have totally different personalities and behavior patterns. Why? Because their response to the same situation is sparked by different feelings. They will relate differently to the same circumstance.

To help understand this concept, let's start by imagining that we respond to ideas, to people, to objects, *and* to situations not for what they are but what they symbolize to us.

What are symbols? They are substitutes, logos, or images of some reality. Words are symbols. The word r-a-i-n will never make us wet. It simply conveys to us a natural and familiar process.

People who become upset about what are called "dirty four-letter words" must remember that it's not the word that upsets them, it's the resistance to the feeling they've chosen to attach to what the word symbolizes.

The caduceus is a symbol of the field of medicine. It is not a license to practice. We take photographs when we travel, so that at home we can show a facsimile of where we've been, a symbol of our experience.

Feelings are no different. They also have symbols. The feeling of celebration needs a symbol to express it. For example, there are many objects or situations we may choose to symbolize the feeling of celebration. Parties, dancing, presents, champagne, ice cream and cake, to name a few. Not everyone will use the same symbol for the same feeling, of course.

Since most of us are not truly in touch with our feelings, we use symbols to bring our feelings to the surface. To be experienced, feelings must be externalized. We lead ourselves to situations in order to act out our feelings. We need situations to see ourselves. We are defined by how we relate to life, and our behavior depends on how we relate to our feelings.

If we have an inner feeling of frustration, we can always lead ourselves to a traffic jam. That way, we have a perfect excuse for our irritation and impatience. We can, that is, unless a traffic jam is not our symbol of frustration. Many a busy Manhattan executive has admitted being delighted to be in traffic, inside a taxi cab, undisturbed. Visitors from a tiny village are most often delighted to be stuck in traffic so they have time to look around. For some, a traffic jam is an annoyance. For others it's an opportunity.

When we say people have things in common, what we're really saying is they have chosen a similar feeling for the same symbol. "We share our love of the beach in common," may mean the beach is my symbol of feeling peaceful, while the beach may symbolize a feeling of freedom for you. The feelings are different, but they are both ones we enjoy. Consequently, we have our love of the beach in common, or more accurately, we have our love of what the beach symbolizes in common.

The same principle applies to things we resist. One person dislikes opera because it symbolizes his feeling of not being good enough. He doesn't understand it and so "not good enough" is what opera means to him. She doesn't like opera because, as a young girl, she was forced to listen to classical music instead of popular, which she loved. Opera, ever since, has become her symbol of feeling controlled. He and she have their dislike of opera in common because he avoids feeling not good enough and she resists feeling controlled.

Let's take a look at how we turn objects into symbols. Children do it all the time, with unashamed delight. Give a youngster a big box and see all the things the box will become or symbolize. For grownups, money is a more complex example, but the process is the same. Money is a myriad of different feeling symbols. To some people it's a symbol of feeling free. To some it's a symbol of feeling important. To others it's a symbol of feeling responsible.

Parents, for some people, are symbols of feeling secure. For others, they are a symbol of feeling obligated.

Our heroes are symbols that we have created. The death of John Fitzgerald Kennedy, Jr., is a perfect example. Most of us didn't know him or had ever met him. He hadn't done anything in his life that would have made him an idol, yet he was a tremendous symbol to much of the world. It seems as though most people thought of JFK, Jr., as the last link to their image of his father and their fantasy of Camelot. When he died in the plane crash, that symbol was gone and there wasn't another suitable symbol around to replace him.

This is the same difficulty for a man who, after his wife dies, says he'll never love again. He turns his wife into a symbol and refuses to choose another symbol for his love.

Personalities like Michael Jordan are symbols for millions of people. We think that if we were Michael Jordan, we'd never have to face feeling unimportant again. So he becomes our symbol of feeling important. The only person we can be sure doesn't use Michael Jordan as this symbol is the man himself. In interviews, he has referred to how often, during his life, he faced feeling unimportant.

The pattern for turning situations into symbols is the same. We may say that our child getting a reward is a situation that makes us happy. However, what is really making us happy is that the reward is a symbol, a mirror of our feeling of pride, validation, good enough, or any feeling we have deemed worth experiencing. We could also choose to be sad by using the situation of his leaving home as a symbol of separation—now he is going out on his own and that symbolizes a feeling of disconnection, loneliness, and emptiness.

Whatever the circumstance, it's the feeling within that affects our lives. Christ said, "The kingdom of heaven is within." In 1927, at the Solvay Congress, Albert Einstein, Neils Bohr,

Max Plank, Werner Heisenberg, and a few other notables came up with what they called "the Copenhagen Interpretation." It said, "Everything *out there* depends on a rigorous mathematical sense, as well as a philosophical one, on what we decide *in here*." Carl Jung said, "When an inner situation (which is a feeling) is not made conscious, it happens outside as coincidence." Whether our belief system is built on Spirit or science (as though science were not also Spirit), the evidence points directly to the fact that our happiness depends entirely on what's inside ourselves, not what we see outside.

If you need more convincing, imagine yourself in the same place with the same people doing the same thing for seven days in a row. Would you have the same feeling all the time? Of course not. The truth is, we do not feel as a result of what we see; we see as a result of what we feel. *A Course in Miracles*, a popular metaphysical book published by The Foundation for Inner Peace, begins its first lesson with the following affirmation: "I have given everything I see all the meaning it has for me." A new twist on the old phrase is, "If I hadn't believed it, I wouldn't have seen it."

Some abused children feel violated by that situation of abuse and remain angry, often for the rest of their lives. Others feel guilty, believing it was their fault. Still others feel compassion and forgive the offender. They see the abuse as a way to help others. This is not an excuse for child abuse, but it shows that even a vicious experience is only what it symbolizes for the one who experiences it.

Everything we see is connected to a feeling behind it, so that what we are seeing is a symbol of our feeling. This is certainly one of the most difficult concepts for us to accept. To say that circumstances *mirror* our feelings rather than *cause* them is not a phrase that rolls easily off the tongue.

If a son is the apple of his father's eye, leaving home could be dad's symbol of loss or disappointment. If the son were seen as a pain in his father's neck, the symbol might be one of celebration or relief. The same object or situation can be a different symbol for different people. Money is a symbol of power to one person and a symbol of responsibility to another. The opposite also applies. Different objects can be the same symbol, and elicit the same feeling. Consider the woman who marries six times, and each time the result is the same. The objects—husbands—have changed, but the symbol—marriage—and the feeling behind it remains the same.

There are times, however, that both twin feelings and their symbols appear simultaneously. Let's look at freedom and confinement. The more freedom we seek, the more confinement we may need to face. Let's suppose that traveling symbolizes freedom (and it does for some people). If they want the freedom of being able to travel from New York to Washington, they will have to be confined in a car, train, or airplane. The faster or farther they want to travel, the more they will be confined. Traveling to the moon requires the most confinement, of course.

Situations being symbols are, therefore, seductive representatives of feelings. No single situation can ever be counted on to elicit a specific feeling. It's common practice to believe that because we would feel *one* way about a situation, the choice of that feeling is universal. How often we are asked, "Well, wouldn't you have felt the same way?" If we don't answer, "yes," the questioner is usually puzzled. When we respond to a situation one way, it's not easy to imagine someone else responding in another. "How could they do that? How can she live like this? What does he see in her?" are just a few of the utterances of disbelief when people respond with a different feeling than what we would have felt. Why? Because we all have different symbols, different feelings for the same happening. If the boss yells at you, and your job is a symbol of security, you will respond quite differently than after a tirade from the "old man," when the job is a symbol of limitation. Your responses to feeling secure and feeling limited are undoubtedly quite different.

Simultaneous Realities

The variety of symbols creates *simultaneous realities*. While most people agree that the Empire State Building is a building, they will not all perceive it in the same way because it represents different symbols, different experiences, and different feelings to different people. The original architects see the building one way. The renting agents see it another. An airplane pilot caught in a pea soup fog over Manhattan sees it yet another. The cleaning woman who sees it only during the quiet hours when everyone else is gone, sees it her way. A man from a small village in Africa who has never seen a building over two stories tall, sees it his way. A couple who are forced to move from New York, the city they love, see it their way. Were all of those people to view the skyscraper at the same time, it would be a perfect example of simultaneous realities.

Scientific View of Reality

Nobel Prize winner Eugene Wigner was once asked to define reality. He answered simply, "Reality is your perception."

The eminent cyberneticist Heinz Von Foester pointed out that the human mind does not perceive what *is* "out there," but what it believes *should be* "out there."

In one of his lectures, physicist John A. Wheeler said, "Out there, there is no light and no color, only electro-magnetic waves. Out there, there is no sound and no music, there are only periodic variations of pressure. Out there, there is no heat or cold, only moving molecules with kinetic energy. We have no evidence that 'out there' exists."

When someone says, "Get real!" they are actually stating the limits of their reality. "Get real!" simply means, "Come into the reality where I can relate to you. Your reality isn't real to me."

New Realities

Irving had been blind since early childhood. At age forty, he consented to have an operation on his eyes. A new surgical technique had been perfected and he was thrilled with the thought of being able to see once again. When the surgeons came in to remove the bandages, they asked Irving to explain what he saw to determine how well he could distinguish shapes. Irving looked at the object he was to describe, and said, "Please, would you let me feel it first?" Even being able to see, he needed his old familiar reality to experience something new.

There are, of course, many common symbols, common realities. One of the best examples is that of the 1929 stock market crash. An untold number of people considered their jobs a symbol of their self-worth. They were the ones who jumped out of the window or otherwise gave up on life. Several, not only killed themselves, but their brokers as well—all over fighting a feeling of worthlessness. Didn't everybody suffer during the Great Depression? Most people did because they had a tremendous attachment to security and an even bigger aversion to insecurity. Some Depression babies are still fighting poverty seventy years later, when they have plenty of money.

However, even when the majority share the same symbol, the same reality, there are always those with something different. Some people suffered the "crash" with a sense of gained self-worth by going through hard times and coming out the other side. Still others *were* able to prosper. One situation and at least four different responses. Four simultaneous realities.

Our modern approach to gender is one example of how we have begun to unify our symbols and our realities. Aggressive/receptive are the twins to notice. Until recently, men were symbols of aggression, while women were the receptive models. No more! At least not in this country. Today, women are heads of corporations and heads of state, which takes more than a tad of aggression. Men are beginning to express their receptive nature. They recognize that allowing themselves to experience softness does not diminish their strength or force in the slightest. They can appear on TV cuddling babies without an affront to their masculinity. Now, truly aware men and women can be aggressive *and* receptive. Having begun to integrate these feeling twins, we are finally going beyond the age-old gender symbols, and now we'll have to find some new ones.

The very latest example of creating a new world of symbols is virtual reality. The illusions seem so real. They are more than three-dimensional and are designed to trick the eye, the ear, and the feelings as well.

This is what Eastern philosophy means by living in a world of illusion. It doesn't mean that the symbols aren't there. It means they are just symbols—reflections—metaphors—forms—part of the play of life. Symbols are not bad things. They are essential. Our only problem with them is when we start believing the symbols are the real thing.

We use objects or activities to symbolize feelings so whatever we are feeling seems appropriate. Many of us use overcast skies as a symbol of sadness. There is nothing intrinsically unhappy about clouds, but it has become an almost universal symbol for lack of enthusiasm.

We spend our lives creating external symbols that reflect our internal feelings. Jobs, possessions, parties, vacations, relationships are all symbols. Everything we see is a symbol of a feeling we have attributed to it. (Each object and situation is a symbol, but the symbol is not the feeling, just as the map is not the territory.) Living through symbols is like seeing the reflection of your loved one in a mirror and trying to have sex with the mirror or trying to destroy a feeling by shooting someone. While you may destroy the person, the symbol, you will never destroy the feeling—feelings are indestructible.

Someone should have mentioned that to the young boys from Columbine High School. Perhaps if they had realized that by doing away with their classmates, they would not have done away with their pain, they wouldn't have gone on such a rampage. The dissemination of this fact, be it from parent to child, from minister to congregation, on TV, over the Internet, or any way it can be sent, might eliminate or at least postpone further avoidable violence.

That's certainly one reason for realizing that happiness and joy are not "out there," not in the symbols. The main reason is that when we discover what feeling the "out there" circumstance or object symbolizes, we can choose any object or circumstance for that feeling. That way, we're always free to elicit the feeling we want, regardless of the circumstance or object.

A process that might help distinguish between feelings and symbols is to begin to notice what objects or situations you use to experience a particular feeling. For example, what symbolizes celebration to you? What symbolizes romance? Then remember it's not the symbol or situation you want. It's the feeling symbolized. Chances are, the cute little restaurant with checked tablecloths, red wine, soft music, and the charming waiter did not mirror the same feeling for you the second or third time you were there.

Once you've recognized your symbol, try replacing it with another symbol. If you're successful, keep changing symbols. You'll be surprised how your feelings become more acute and recognizable, and how the symbols are relegated to just what they are—symbols. For example, if your main symbol of celebration is champagne, pick another symbol, then another until you no longer have to suffer from a hangover after celebrating. If, even after repeated attempts, you're unable to change or add another symbol—*stop.* You *are* attached to that symbol. That's okay. At least you'll never be frustrated by having to make choices or be bothered with the nuisance of endless alternatives.

✦ ✦ ✦

Whatever we see
"out there" is a clear mirror
of what is "in here."

CHAPTER 4

✦ ✦ ✦

Thinking Is Not Feeling

Feelings lead us not only into situations but into thought patterns as well. Now that we've distinguished feelings from situations, we'll do the same thing with feelings and thoughts. Thinking is what we do to give a story line to our feelings. For instance, very few of us can sit silently and experience the feeling of being excluded without some image in mind. We usually connect the feeling with an incident or an imagined scenario, and then logically conclude that the thought produced the feeling. Consider that it might be the other way around. The feeling leads to the thought, which is created in order to justify the feeling. "Free-floating anxiety" is when we are resisting the feeling of fear but haven't yet come up with a specific symbol or thought that we can use to justify it.

It's true that we often hear, "Every time I think of him, I feel vengeful," as though the feeling came from the thought. However, it's that subconscious stirring of the feeling of vengeance that leads to the thought. Not vice-versa. We certainly connect more than one feeling with each memory. The reason that one is more prevalent is that it is the one we need to investigate at the moment.

✦ ✦ ✦

Reminder: Accepting that the feeling precedes the thought, may be a new concept, but it is definitely worth exploring. Why? Because if feelings bring about thoughts and we can make friends with the feelings, there won't be a thought in the world that can disturb us.

✦ ✦ ✦

If the feeling is fear,
the thought could be, "What will happen if I get sick?"

If the feeling is disappointment,
the thought could be, "Now I can't go to the party."

If the feeling is discouragement,
the thought could be, "I'll never learn computers."

If the feeling is anger,
the thought could be, "He had no right to yell at me."

Someone with no fear of illness will choose another symbol of fear, one of their own choosing to exercise the feeling. Someone who considers illness an inconvenience may have a thought pattern that leads more to the disappointment area. "Now, I'll miss out on (fill in the blank)." If discouragement is the number one priority, the thought may go more like, "Why is it that every time I get close to finishing this project, I get sick?" Anger produces thought like, "Why me?"

The thought fits the feeling like a glove. It's the impetus for the action that follows. There would have been, however, no thought without the feeling that proceeded it.

How about thoughts like, "$E = mc^2$"? What feeling could possibly be behind a totally intellectual thought like that? There could be several. If you're saying it to prove a point, it could be a feeling of validation. If you're saying it to show that you're aware, it may be a feeling of pride. If you're saying it for the first time, it might be a feeling of discovery. There can be many symbols or thoughts that represent one feeling, just as there can be many feelings that are represented by a symbol or a thought.

This concept may take a little getting used to at first, but once you begin to notice how often your thinking revolves around a feeling you want or want to avoid, you'll start to get the hang of it. The feeling of insecurity presents a clear example. People who fight insecurity are plagued with thoughts of their supposed enemy all the time. In fact, almost everything seems to reflect the fear. Nothing at all has to happen for the thought, the image to arise. As long as the fear is there, as long as we have a feeling, we will usually come up with an appropriate mental scenario.

How many times do we ask ourselves, "Where did that thought come from?" Now you might try asking yourself "What feeling is generating this thought?" Stream-of-consciousness thinking is often used in therapy to allow our thoughts to lead us to the feelings behind the thinking. Doctors William Gray and Paul La Violette reported in the March 1982 edition of the *Brain/Mind Bulletin*, "Feelings are the matrix of all thought." For example, when you think you want to lose weight, but your number one priority, your feeling, is to avoid the feeling of missing out, your mind will reflect nothing but the food you'll be missing.

Most of us try to manipulate thinking, believe it or not, as an attempt to avoid a feeling. When faced with a feeling we are trying to skirt, it's not unusual to say to ourselves, "I'll just think of something else." It never works, at least for any length of time, but it's a habit we repeat over and over. Look at Scarlet O'Hara's vow to think about it tomorrow at Tara. What we are all saying, in effect, is that we want to get out of what we are feeling in this moment.

Therein lies a very destructive practice. Anything we do to deny this moment is denying part of our lives. Dashing off to the future, stumbling back to the past, or pretending the present is something other than what it is leaves us in no man's land. As we have seen, we need both up and down, in and out, expansion and contraction to exist. Making believe we can live with only positive energy is, at the very least, totally unrealistic. The plethora of positive thinking preached by many of the New Agers is not thought as much as it is a fantasy. It is not new. It is antediluvian. People have been trying to cover up their pain with happy thoughts since the great flood.

Accentuating one side of a polarity in order to eliminate the other, is the height of the addiction/aversion syndrome. It also builds the aggressive boundaries of dualism: the mine-infested path that glorifies the acceptable, while attempting to destroy all that is unacceptable. We all have greedy, aggressive, insensitive thoughts. If we didn't we could never have generous, receptive, sensitive, harmonious ones. To deny the former is to lose the latter. All the world's prophets must have been aware of this since there has never been a record of Jesus, Buddha, Moses, Lao Tzu, Mohammed, or any other wise person running around shouting, "Think positive!"

It has been said, "As a man thinketh in his heart, so is he." When we think with our hearts, we feel. To try to change our unwanted thoughts without changing our fight with our feelings, is like putting a clean bandage over an infected wound. Changing our thoughts will do nothing without changing what's beneath them. We may think our way to a temporary success, but we must feel our way to joy and bliss.

✦ ✦ ✦

*The answer to life's
most fundamental questions
lies between the thoughts.*

CHAPTER 5

Be Careful
What You Ask For

This chapter moves to the very core of running to the angels or from the goblins. It deals with questions like, "What's the difference between wanting to feel valid, and wanting to avoid feeling invalid?" One answer could certainly be, "Just the quality of your life." That's all. The answer to the question, "Isn't wanting to feel important the same as wanting to avoid feeling unimportant?" would be, "As similar as happiness and unhappiness."

Wanting to experience a feeling is like running to the angels. If we have a clear commitment and the patience, we'll eventually find them. Wanting to avoid a feeling is like running from the goblins, and that is a lifetime career. The goblins will be forever chasing us, and no one has yet outrun them.

There appears to be a universal law that states: You always get the feeling you want or the feeling you want to avoid, whichever want is stronger. If we want to run toward angels, angels will be on our horizon. If we want to run from goblins, there will be a goblin in fast pursuit.

Rest assured that this law does not refer to situations. The desire to avoid a cold in no way depletes our immune system. However, resisting feeling dependent does lead to circumstances where independence flies out the window. Why? We're back to the benevolent universe giving us exactly what we request. If we want to fight feeling dependent, we will be faced with all kinds of situations where we can do just that.

If we commit to fight feeling threatened, we might find one tyrannical boss after another. We'll keep leading ourselves to bosses, or friends, or even a mate, who will keep threatening us so we can keep fighting feeling threatened. Even if they don't actually threaten us, we'll conveniently think that's what they're doing, so we can keep fighting the same old feeling. We will have gotten the very thing to which we were committed—fighting feeling threatened. This could be one explanation of "what we resist persists."

Any time we commit to fighting a feeling, we see every situation that comes along as a God-given opportunity to do just that. This is why difficult situations that seem to be challenges, problems, or even punishments are often our desire to battle with a feeling. Consequently, we find ourselves at war and seldom notice that we are at least partially responsible for the encounter. When we try to avoid feeling not good enough, we wonder why everyone who looks at us seems to be judging us below standard. Whether they are or not doesn't seem to matter. Our commitment to resistance takes over and everything we see mirrors our need to resist.

Nowhere is taking responsibility for our own feelings more important than in a marriage. The need to blame a spouse for our feelings is hands down the biggest cause of divorce, separation, and marital unrest. There have been endless numbers of books written about husbands' and wives' responsibility for family duties. Courses are given all over the world helping couples rearrange family responsibilities. There are times when it's necessary for the woman to be the breadwinner of the family. There are times when the man is required to take over the household chores. Any responsibility can be shifted from one partner to another; any one, that is, except for feelings.

No one can be responsible for another's feelings. As Eleanor Roosevelt once said, "No one can make you happy or sad without your permission." The happiest couples are the ones who never blame one another for the way they feel. The most successful boss/employee relationships flourish when both accept the responsibility for the way they feel.

What about the couple where there is certainly just cause for blame? Let's say, one is extremely abusive. We must remember that with the exception of the few remaining societies where marriages are planned by the parents, the bride and groom have chosen each other. There was some reason they both wanted the union. Often—unfortunately—one was supposed to be the savior in helping the other avoid a feeling. The fantasy was that the designated savior would not only keep away the feeling but would take the blame if the mission was not accomplished. Since, as we have said, "No one can make us feel something, or stop us from feeling," a marriage like this is doomed before the vows are taken. This is why marriages based on "He will save me from feeling insecure," or "She will keep me from feeling lonely" never work. No partnership will work as long as one is blamed for another's feelings. We are experiencing, or resisting, a feeling because that's what we've committed to do.

How do we know our commitment? We're not always aware of exactly what it is. Sometimes our commitments appear to be made almost subconsciously. Discovering the feeling we've asked for is never a difficult or complicated task. It's found by telling ourselves just what we're feeling at the moment. That's it! That's all! What we're feeling is exactly what we've decided to feel. Whatever feeling we've decided to fight, whether we're aware of the decision or not, is just what we're doing. It's not the situation's fault, it's not our spouse's fault, it's not society's fault, it's not the government's fault, it's not God's fault. There is no fault. There is no blame. If we want to change the feeling, or the fight, all we have to do is ask. Whom do we ask? The person who is doing the fighting or the feeling, of course.

✦　✦　✦

If we cannot find
anything to upset us,
we'll make something up.

CHAPTER 6

✦ ✦ ✦

What Do You Mean, Attached to Our Aversions?

One of the reasons the English language is so difficult to learn is that there are so many words that mean the same thing. There are countless ways of saying, "We'll all be happier when we can let go of our aversions." As a matter of fact, we're taking a whole chapter to say just that—and we won't have even scratched the surface.

The person learning English also has to cope with the challenge of one word, or one phrase, having several different meanings. Let's take the phrase "letting go." For some people it means "getting rid of." For others it means "giving away." The letting go we speak of has neither of these two meanings.

When we hear a person shouting, "Let go!" we can usually be sure the person they're addressing is holding on to something. This is the letting go to which we are referring. In this book, "letting go" means simply "stop holding on." More specifically, stop holding onto our *resistance to a feeling*.

Getting back to the challenge of different words with the same approximate meaning: Over the years, we've discovered that the word "resistance" has a large charge for most people.

We've decided to use the word "aversion" instead. It means the same thing and seems more user-friendly. We will also use the word "avoidance," with the same connotation in mind.

However, before we deal with any of them, let's start with their polarities: "attachment," "identification," and "addiction."

Attachments

Three of the world's philosophies go so far as to suggest that all of our suffering comes from our attachment *to* and the identification *with* anything. When we say "attached," we recognize that there's quite a difference between being involved and being attached. We can be involved without becoming attached. We can be involved in a project without being attached to the outcome. Most of the things we do for pleasure are done for the fun of the process, and the end result is secondary. A great conversation is one where all participants discover something, enjoy the exchange, and are not concerned about how it ends.

An actor may completely involve himself in rehearsals, developing the role and performing his best. Then, if a critic criticizes what he's done, he can either learn from it and go on with the performances, or he can be attached to what the readers must think of him, and agonize over every review. The more he can let go, the better his subsequent performances will be, and the longer his career will last.

Identification With

When we say "being identified" with something, we're using it in the same manner as being attached to it. The man who says he's not attached to his job will readily admit he identifies with it. He sees himself as an executive. That's the role he plays. That way, when he retires and no longer has that role, or identification, there is often a real crisis. To give you an idea of how critical this particular crisis has become, according to a recent report, the average lifespan of a retired executive is *two* years.

Addictions

While "attachment" is usually considered a rather benign word, its synonym "addiction" is not. To be attached to something is to be unable to separate or unable to get along without whatever it is we are attached to. Seems a lot like an addiction, doesn't it? Although attachment may sound less offensive, it still implies the parasitic lack of freedom. Mushrooms and orchids are delicious and beautiful, but they need a host to exist. When we become attached to something *it* becomes *our* host and we feel we can't be a happy person without it. We are addicted to having it around and need it for our sense of ourselves. We've all known people who thought they owned something and were so addicted to it we said it owned them.

Because of substance abuse, addiction has become a particularly loaded word. While it is still something we wish to let go, in severe cases of drug abuse, for example, a simple letting go, or stopping "cold turkey," is not always possible. Letting go might have to be gradual, since a sudden release could be fatal. The point to remember is that the original addiction was the result of an attachment, not to a substance but to a feeling that substance represented.

One problem we're not always aware of is how strongly we are attached, addicted to, or identified with any feeling. The following list of four feelings and the attachments, identifications, and addictions that accompany them is an effort to help us see exactly where we are stuck. Almost all of our discomfort falls under one of these four headings.

1. *Fear* accompanies the attachment *to* and identification *with* standards and security.

2. *Disappointment* accompanies the attachment *to* and identification *with* expectations and gratification.

3. *Discouragement* accompanies the attachment *to* and identification *with* completion and purpose.

4. *Anger* accompanies the attachment *to* and identification *with* perception and appreciation.

Letting Go

Letting go of attachments, identification, and addictions is not a simple thing to do. Of all the courageous acts a person can perform, probably the most challenging is letting go. Once we have become attached to something, it's as though we are gripping it with our fists. The stronger the attachment, the tighter the grip. Then when the time comes to let it go, to loosen the grip, the muscles, having been so contracted for a long time, go into spasm. However, the pain is necessary if we're ever to use that hand again. In fact, the pain is the cure, for without the temporary discomfort of loosening the grip, the fist would stay clenched forever and the muscles would eventually atrophy.

We need to remember that the letting go we're talking about is not letting go of possessions, or ideas, but rather our *addiction to* those possessions and ideas. For example, we often insist that the universe present us with exactly the experiences we demand. Our expectations must be met. Our standards must be reached and end results achieved, and everyone must see us precisely the way we want to be seen. We want these self-created rules to be recognized and respected. We are addicted to them. Unfortunately the universe doesn't always respond to our demands. It moves quietly on in its gentle and ever-changing way, while we are left flailing and fussing, crying and complaining.

Aversions

As forceful as attachments and addictions may sound, they are only part of the story, and the smallest part of the story, at that. Aversions are the real culprits that we refuse to let go. Addictions and aversions are two different views of the same thing. When we say, "Addictions are things we can't live without," we could just as easily say, "Aversions are things we can't live with." Our addiction to getting something is the same as our aversion to being without it. Being addicted to having our own way is also having an aversion to *not* having our own way. An addiction is an aversion to not getting what we want.

If addictions and aversions are interchangeable words, why do we spend more time on aversions? Because they are more prevalent. Believe it or not, there are more things in life to which we have aversions than ones to which we are addicted. We are more a society of avoiders than of acceptors. What most people think of as their attachments are really aversions in disguise. If you doubt it, ask your friends and family to make a list of all the things they love and another list of all the things they'd love to avoid. We'll bet that in almost every case the first list will be a great deal shorter.

The reason for all this attention to our aversions is that *aversion is where our power lies.* It can be aptly said we are attached to our aversions. It's not the attachment to shopping for expensive clothes that runs up our credit cards; it's the aversion to feeling below standard in what we usually wear.

When someone's aversion to a feeling of inadequacy becomes overwhelming, that's when they rush out and buy a two-hundred-dollar pair of shoes that will probably remain in the closet unworn. Whenever some people's aversion to feeling powerless gets out of hand, they scream at their employees.

We always get what we want, *or what we* want to avoid, *whichever* want *is stronger.* For most people, being well is not the priority, avoiding being sick is. With this in mind, it's not surprising that the percentage of ill people is climbing daily. Since the number one priority is fighting illness, not being healthy, the benevolent universe is quick to provide us with illness so that we can fight it. Most people don't want to be rich as much as they want to avoid being poor. It's amazing the number of people who go to parties more to avoid feeling excluded than to enjoy the festivities. People who are addicted to being right have an even greater aversion to being wrong.

The attachment to winning is well recognized and highly promoted in our society. Again, it's not so much the ecstasy of winning, as it is *avoiding* the agony of losing. We're back to the Olympic silver medalists who didn't feel the ecstacy of being a silver medalist but felt the agony of not getting the gold.

Not being a loser is the impetus for the extra exertion in every field from high school football to the Fortune 500 companies. According to the American Heart Association, it is the impetus for a large percentage of heart attacks as well.

One reason for the lack of success in many substance-abuse programs is the small amount of attention paid to the aversion behind the addiction. As a matter of fact, the addiction to a substance is really an aversion to what we would feel without the substance. An addiction, in the strictest sense, is temporary relief from an aversion. Some people drink to drown their aversion to the feeling of inadequacy. Others "shoot up" to repress their aversion to the feeling of boredom. Still others light a cigarette to soothe their aversion to the feeling of being pressured. Consequently, the difficulty with many rehab programs is that they attempt to eliminate the addiction, which is a kind of friend, while leaving the aversion untouched, unexposed, and festering.

The only reason for the majority of addictions is to temporarily relieve an aversion. So trying to eliminate an addiction without addressing the aversion underneath is not only futile, it's downright cruel. It's like seeing a child in pain and taking away the toy that's giving comfort so that the child never becomes addicted to the toy.

We knew one man who, having been addicted to alcohol, kicked the habit only to take up drugs. They provided the needed relief from his aversion to feeling he was missing out. He applied the same steps and group support he had used with alcohol and got off the drugs. Within a month he had simply traded in cocaine for an incredible bout with sugar. His consumption became so intense that he finally developed diabetes and died. His aversion was never resolved. As a result, he struggled from one addiction to another without every finding a cure. When we are able to let go of our aversions, the addictions seem to take care of themselves.

Hypochondriacs rarely enjoy their health. They are always immersed in their aversion to illness. They constantly fear that illness might be just around the corner. A miser doesn't find peace in his possessions. The aversion to losing them far outweighs the satisfaction of having them. In short, the pleasure derived from an addiction is always short lived since the aversion behind it keeps the experience from being much fun.

We had a client, a mature, single woman who confided in us that what she really wanted was a man who loved her so much he couldn't live without her. That way she would never have to face his leaving her and her aversion to feeling abandoned. When we suggested she was not looking for a lover, but someone with such an aversion that he was an emotional cripple, she was appalled. She had never seen that what she thought of as her heart's desire was really an aversion.

The following list is another way of looking at the one we saw a few pages ago. The only difference is this one focuses directly on the aversion behind the addictions.

1. The aversion to feeling *insecure* is accompanied by *fear.*

2. The aversion to feeling *unfulfilled* is accompanied by *disappointment.*

3. The aversion to feeling *incomplete* is accompanied by *discouragement.*

4. The aversion to feeling *unappreciated* is accompanied by *anger.*

The reason for these lists is to help us recognize where our emotional fight really lies. If we are experiencing fear, we might check and see if we are dealing with an aversion to being below standard or to insecurity. If we experience disappointment, chances are some expectation hasn't been met. A glitch of discouragement may be a clue that we are facing something to do with incompletion and a lack of purpose.

The lists, like any lists, are fingers pointing to the moon. They are *not* the moon. They are used to further exemplify the nature and scope of feelings. Once we are aware of our aversion to specific feelings, we then have the choice of continuing our pattern or making a change.

If aversions are the real cause of our discontent, why did we mention addictions in the first place? It's astonishing how many people will listen to how addicted or attached they are to someone or something, but will turn off instantly when it is suggested they have an aversion or a resistance. In our seminars, time and time again, people say they couldn't understand the difference between wanting to feel included and fighting feeling excluded. It sometimes took ages for them to see that running to the angels was not the same as running from the goblins. They claimed, as many still do, that they had no aversion or resistance—they were only protecting against something. It's a shock when we realize all protection rackets are a nice way of saying "aversions" or "resistance."

Why do we develop these aversions to feelings in the first place? One of the biggest reasons is our terror of getting stuck in a feeling, once it is accepted. Please be assured and comforted to know that no one ever gets stuck in a feeling—but may get stuck in a fight with one. We never hear of anyone getting stuck in feeling free. Why then, should we believe that we can be stuck in feeling confined? We can, of course, become stuck in *fighting* feeling confined. That's when we feel trapped. Accepting is opening, while resisting is closing. We never get stuck feeling open, only when we close down and fight feeling confined are we unable to move on to the next experience.

The Garden of Feelings

The garden of feelings is varied and plentiful. It's an exquisite sight to behold. There are flowers for all occasions, and blossoms for every taste. Only our addiction/aversion can limit the bouquets. One hint from some old-time gardeners, practiced at tilling the soil of our feelings: Fussing at the symbol of our aversion will never relieve the aversion. No matter how loud, or how long we scream, "I hate my mother," or "my father," or "my boss," the aversion will not disappear. It hasn't helped so far, has it? This is because mother, or whomever, despite all the protestations, is not the culprit. What we really hate is the feeling, of which mother, father, or the boss, are only the symbols. Perhaps it's the feeling of misunderstood or betrayed—whatever we resist and use mother and company to symbolize. Once we can scream, "I hate feeling unappreciated," we will have taken the first step toward peace. That is the source, the only war that is being fought.

Once we have identified the conflict, we have a choice. We can continue the war, or work toward the peace. There is no criticism of either choice. One is equally as good as another. It all depends on what our priorities happen to be. Once we've made a commitment to go beyond the war, the outcome will mirror it. If our commitment is to experience more of life, as much of it as possible, that's what we'll experience. We will, however, have to let go of our addictions and aversions.

When we can let go of our aversion to feeling mistaken, we'll find that making mistakes often leads us to information that we'd never have had otherwise. Letting go of our aversion to feeling insecure opens us up to experiences totally unavailable in a protected life. Allowing ourselves to miss out on our expectations leaves us free to sense adventures that would otherwise have been impossible. In short, there are greater things in life than we have ever dreamed, if we are willing to take the chance. We can have it all if we're willing to experience and accept it all.

✦ ✦ ✦

No one has ever
found oneness by destroying
half of who they are.

CHAPTER 7

The Big Four:
Fear, Disappointment,
Discouragement, and Anger

As we move into the very core of feelings, let us summarize some key points we have covered so far. Since this is a new paradigm for many, the clearer you will be able to see these points, the easier it will be to move into the practical applications of them.

Key Points

- Chapter 1: All human behavior is built on feelings.
- Chapter 2: Feelings come in pairs. We can't have one feeling while blocking its twin. Resisting feelings never gets us what we want.
- Chapter 3: Circumstances do not cause feelings. They simply symbolize the feelings that we are accepting or resisting.
- Chapter 4: Thoughts also mirror feelings, not the other way around.

- Chapter 5: You always get the feeling you want or the feeling you want to avoid, whichever want is stronger.
- Chapter 6: Addictions are just another way of looking at aversions.
- Chapter 7: The message of this chapter is that we generally relate to situations in one of four ways.

Yes! You've read all this before. However, there is a reason for the repetition of these ideas, along with several others in the book. It is not accidental, or an oversight. It's the suggestion of a very wise minister who said, "If you want people to remember something, tell it to them three times. First, you tell them what you're going to tell them. Then you tell them. Then you tell them what you've told them." So forgive the repetition. If you've got the point, move right along.

Pinpointing Our Feelings

When we are fighting feeling not good enough, we'll experience fear. We may show it or not, and we may manifest the fight in different ways. Some of us will operate like a steamroller in an attempt to prove that we have successfully avoided feeling not good enough. Others will function from a shy, retiring place and be unwilling to try things for fear of experiencing that very feeling.

Most of us not yet fluent with our feelings, often find it hard to tell them apart, and even then, the list seems endless. That's why we have, hopefully, simplified the job by dividing feelings into four categories. They are mentioned in the previous chapter, and are important enough that each will have its own individual chapter later on. For now, let's consider that almost all feelings we experience, fall under one of four big categories:

✦ ✦ ✦

Reminder: You may be used to seeing everything reduced to just fear, or reduced to just anger. The four categories are not the last word on the human psyche, but they are a very useful mechanism for discovery, understanding, acceptance, and growth. Apply them, even if your old paradigm was different. See what happens. Each category will present new insights to explore.

✦ ✦ ✦

Fear, Disappointment, Discouragement, Anger

Let's begin with *fear*. Suppose we want to avoid feeling insecure. If something comes along to threaten our security, what happens? Fear happens. The more insecurity we feel, the more we fight, the stronger the fear. It can be anywhere from mild concern to absolute panic. When fear is happening, there is probably resistance to, or a rejection of, one of the following sets of feelings. Insecurity is only one of the many possibilities. Fear is the *clue* that guides you to this list to identify one of the specific twins you are rejecting. This also pinpoints where the acceptance can set you free.

adequate/inadequate   secure/insecure
independent/dependent   special/average
good enough/not good enough perfect/imperfect
successful/unsuccessful   superior/inferior
prepared/unprepared   worthy/unworthy

When *disappointment* is happening, it is a clue to your possible resistance to one of the following feeling twins:

abundant/lacking   full/empty
creative/uncreative   gain/loss
stimulated/unstimulated   limitless/limited
free/confined   wanted/unwanted

If *discouragement* is your Armageddon, the chances are your battle is with one of these:

organized/disorganized   complete/incomplete
productive/unproductive   effective/ineffective
purposeful/purposeless   focused/unfocused
important/unimportant

You will notice that the next, *anger,* by far the most familiar, is the longest list. Despite all the books written about fear being the cause of most pain and discomfort, there appears to be more anger happening than any other of the big four. It has been suggested that anger is merely a cover-up for fear. However, we've all seen people creating such rage that it would be hard to imagine fear being even a minuscule part. Whether or not fear and anger are from one and the same stem, for the purpose of this process, let's just let them each be one of four siblings. Then, no matter how much they resemble one another, *we* will be able to tell them apart.

When anger is happening, it is time to investigate its core cause, an attempt to avoid one or more of the following:

acknowledged/overlooked   noticed/unnoticed
agreed with/challenged   powerful/powerless
appreciated/unappreciated   right/wrong
connected/disconnected   special/ordinary
understood/misunderstood   validated/invalidated
victimized/fairly treated   included/excluded

There are overlaps, of course. Some people have a *fear* of being average, while others become downright *angry* at being referred to as ordinary or average. There is no hard and fast rule. These are simply fingers pointing to the moon. They are possible feelings to which we have an aversion, ones that we are denying, fighting, or trying to destroy. The list certainly does not approach being complete. It is deceptively small, but comparatively universal.

The Four Areas of Our Lives

The four major categories—fear, disappointment, discouragement, and anger—are furthermore correlated to the four major areas of our lives:

1. *Fear*: our relationship to who we are.

2. *Disappointment:* our relationship to what we have.

3. *Discouragement:* our relationship to what we do.

4. *Anger:* our relationship to others.

Our approach to life is built on these four areas. As tiny babies, our first concern was with who we were. Many of us, to this day, are still pondering that question. As we grew, so did our attachment to the *things* we had acquired. Later, as we matured, we became more concerned with what we were doing. Our final area of interest was with other people and how we related to them.

The areas of *being-having-doing-connecting* with others have been the four areas of growth, maturity, and increasing awareness. Consequently, they are the areas where we encounter the most difficulty, the most discomfort, and the most confusion.

Since our entire life is governed by our relationship with ourselves, with things around us, with our activities, and with others, we might compare these relationships to the four rooms of our house of behavior. Most of us spend a lot more time in one room than in the others. For some, the self room is seldom used and the possession room is crammed to the ceiling. For others, the achievement/accomplishment room gets all the traffic. For still others, the only really comfortable room is the one filled with lots of people.

All of us visit all four rooms daily. All of us sweep and clean, laugh and play, cry and hide all over the house. All of us have one room, or at least a corner of one room that we've put off limits and neglected. It's a place we don't like that we've tried to avoid, deny, and even destroy.

Well, that's where we're going. We're going to clean up that place, let the light in, take a good look at it and find out how beautiful it *really* is. Once that's done, we can promise you, without a doubt, that the whole house will look and feel a lot better.

The four different feeling patterns also mirror the way we relate. The four different feelings cause us to create four different ways of relating. When we are dealing with security/ insecurity, good enough/not good enough, and so forth, the manner in which we relate will be all about *being*. When our feelings are about abundance/lack, empty/full, etc., our relating will center around *having*. When we are experiencing feelings of complete/incomplete, purposeful/purposeless, and so forth, we will be concerned with *doing*. Right/wrong, validated/invalidated, understood/misunderstood, and so forth, will all lead to situations about *connection*.

An Apology

In our first book, *Let Go & Live*, we made the grave mistake of labeling people who habitually fell into one of the four feeling patterns. We referred to them as a *be-er*, a *haver*, a *doer*, or a *connector*. We humbly admit we were mistaken. We forgot that giving names, labels, or categories to anything diminishes what is named. Perhaps that's why the book is out of print. The moment we label anything, we will ever after think of it in connection with its label. That label becomes a symbol and none of us changes symbols lightly. Labeling limits our discovery of the total thing we've labeled. There is an old Zen saying that the moment you teach a child the word, "dog," it will never see a dog the same way again.

The talented figure skater, Brian Orser, is now always introduced as, "The two-time silver medalist, Brian Orser." It's as though he *is* his medals. He is identified with them, and when we see him, we're supposed to think "medals."

Consequently, we are faced with a dilemma: how to present the four behavior patterns without putting boundaries around them or becoming identified with any one of them. Words tend to freeze reality, and yet we need words to communicate. So, we'll do the best we can to help identify our feelings without thinking that our feelings identify who we are. Perhaps we can think of them as modes in which we relate, so we're free to switch how we relate as we switch feelings.

We can notice indications of specific modes of being in everyday situations. For example, if a friend has a baby, and we are in a *being* mode, we will probably buy the child something like a silver cup or spoon. That way we would not have to be afraid of being below standard. If we were in a *having* mode, we'd probably present the little tyke with a humongous teddy bear, to be sure not to disappoint him or have him miss out. If our *doing* mode was paramount, the child would undoubtedly receive something like a savings bond, for a long-term purpose. The *connecting* mode would elicit a gift of the latest baby-rearing book or something concerned with the "right" way to raise a child.

Everything we do, from giving baby presents to dealing with death, has to do with how we respond to our feelings. At this point, we've hopefully clarified the process of resisting feelings. One word of caution: watch out for being in a hurry to get rid of resistance. If you fuss about your rejecting a feeling, you're just compounding the felony, resisting your resistance, or rejecting your rejections. This is the time for watching. Notice where you give away your peace of mind, your awareness, and your enjoyment of life.

Why Pinpoint Feelings?

Pinpointing the feelings we're resisting is not only helpful in our day-to-day living, but it can help with problems of huge proportions. Illness is probably the most important. After working with two thousand cancer patients, we discovered that, when confronted with the questions of their worst feeling nightmare, the universal answer was "not good enough." This is, of course, not saying that fighting "not good enough" causes cancer. That would be absurd. We're merely suggesting that the chances are, a cancer patient has a very strong aversion to that feeling.

The good news is that accepting the feeling of not good enough has a surprisingly beneficial effect. We have even, in rare cases, seen the patient completely healed. This is why it's important to know which feeling is being fought and depleting the energy that could otherwise be applied to healing.

The following is a list of ten illnesses and the feelings, once accepted, that can release more energy toward a cure:

1. Accepting feeling disconnected helps with allergies.
2. Accepting feeling out of control helps with Alzheimer's disease.
3. Accepting feeling inflexible helps with arthritis.
4. Accepting feeling not good enough helps with cancer.
5. Accepting feeling missing out helps with colitis.
6. Accepting feeling limited helps with diabetes.
7. Accepting feeling misunderstood helps with epilepsy.
8. Accepting feeling powerless helps with asthma.
9. Accepting feeling helpless helps with paralysis.
10. Accepting feeling unaccomplished helps with ulcers.

✦ ✦ ✦

Reminder: There is no bacteria more damaging than continued *aversion and rejection; no medicine stronger than acceptance and respect. The greatest headache possible is the collision of two opposing thoughts. So, whether you accept this list or not, is not important. The greatest cure is not having to agree with others, just allowing them to disagree with you.*

✦ ✦ ✦

It's healthy to remember that illness, like everything else in life, has its place. Illness is sometimes the best and shortest way to learn a lesson. Sometimes people learn though health, sometimes through illness. Sometimes illness and the self-searching that follows is most beneficial. It's also well to remember that without illness there would be no healing. To invent one is to create the other.

This is certainly not to suggest the elimination of medical research or the astonishing discovery of the secrets of the human body. It is only to suggest that many forms of pain and discomfort might be more thoroughly investigated before war is immediately and unconditionally declared. Most members of the American Medical Association agree that the human body is still the most incredible healing machine on the planet. Yet, no doctor in the world can cure a patient who would rather die than face a feeling that is detested.

Illness is the body's way of showing us that something is out of balance, blocked, or rejected. To eliminate the symptom without restoring the balance, or letting go of the fight, is to insure another illness, or that illness' return. Pinpointing just where resistance lies, is certainly one way to restore balance, both emotionally and physically.

Pinpointing feelings is also a way of explaining difficult concepts. Werner Heisenberg's theory of not being able to separate the experiment from the experimenter is more easily understood when we remember that we all lead ourselves to situations so that we can relate to a specific feeling. Let's suppose then, that one experimenter needs to experience success, while the other needs to experience failure. Those feelings will indeed affect the experiment.

The depth of our relationships also depends on our ability to pinpoint our feelings and our resistance to them. If you have a resistance to imperfection, and I have a resistance to incompletion, we're going to face some difficulty before we get things done.

Being able to recognize our attachments to our aversions, helps us in every area of our lives. It influences our health, our work, our social life, every thought we have and every action we take.

✦ ✦ ✦

Our greatest act is
pretending that our act is
not really an act.

No Bad Feelings!
PART II

✦ ✦ ✦

CHAPTER 8

The Art of Being

(Fear—I Am What I Am and I'm Afraid It's Not Good Enough)

Fear. The great black-hooded, unknown that shakes our limbs and makes our blood run cold. The great power of this all-too-familiar monster is that it *is* the unknown. We're never afraid of the moment. It's the future that looms ominously. The fact that we know half the things we worry about never happen, doesn't seem to help a bit. We still worry. We are sometimes hounded by the two-headed Hydra—"what if" and "if only." Our worries may appear to be about some catastrophic happening, but like all situations, our concern boils down to a feeling. It's not really what might happen, as much as, if it does, will we be able to handle it emotionally? Will we be good enough, and if we aren't will we be able to accept that fact? For those of us with an aversion in the *being* mode, the answer is a definite *no!*

There are an astonishing number of people who have created the scenario that if they lose their job, or the stock market adjusts too much, they'll be "bag people." Millions and millions of well-to-do people harbor this fear.

Allyson, a fairly young woman who is separated from her husband, has almost two million dollars in investments, and an annual income in the six figures. She is often terrorized with dreams of becoming a bag lady. All a vivid picture of her resistance to inadequacy. This may seem, to most of us, as totally unrealistic. However, fear has never claimed to be rational. We often see other people's worries as unnecessary, while ours, of course, are quite real.

The basis of all fear is viewing the future and picking the most unacceptable alternative possible. That alternative is the expression or the symbol of a feeling to which we have a terrifying aversion. Rest assured that while we may not be able to prevent the situation, we are always able to accept and integrate the feeling. That way, no matter what happens, or what *might* happen, fear would no longer be a problem.

Even as we accept our feelings, fear will never totally disappear—nor should it. We need fear for balance. We also need fear for fun. The elimination of fear would mean the end of a great deal of suspense, and certainly none of us would vote for that. The excitement of the possibility of danger in entertainment and sports would surely be a loss. Let's face it, a lot of the exhilaration and thrill of life would be gone. The idea is not to dissolve our fear or control it but to—believe it or not—enjoy it. One simple way to enjoy fear is to share it. Once we have admitted our feeling, it takes on an entirely different perspective.

That perspective includes courage. We need fear if we're to have courage. Without fear, courage is meaningless.

Alan was a charming but shy man, especially when it came to speaking in public. One evening he had to address a group of six hundred people. He arrived at the speaker's platform trembling, wondering how he was ever going to survive. He put his hand up to his chest to make sure he was still breathing and inadvertently touched his speaker's badge. From somewhere deep inside his consciousness, he looked at the crowd and said, "This badge says 'Guest Speaker.' It should say, 'The Red Badge of Courage.' Frankly I'm terrified. I'm not sure that I'm qualified to tell you the things you need to hear, but at least I'll give it a try. So bear with me." It was not only the easiest speech he had ever made, but he got a standing ovation at the end. The audience consisted of six hundred mastectomy survivors. They knew what it meant to embrace fear and keep on moving.

Fear is exciting as long as we remember it's here to be experienced not to be judged. Although fear may never be our first choice for feelings, it *can* be a good friend. That way, it will allow us to be friends with its twin: trust.

Trust

Trust is not faith in the future or belief in the past, but trust in the right now—at this very moment. We all need to trust something, even if we trust that there's nothing trustworthy. Trust is not limited to God, Allah, Christ, or any dogma that accompanies them. Trust includes concepts, formulas, equations, theories and all manner of information. Some people trust that there is a universal plan. Others trust that there is no such thing.

There is, however, one thing that most all of us trust. That is, that there is some force, some power, some consciousness that is bigger and more aware than we are. It's comforting to trust that we're not in charge of everything and that all the ills of the world do not fall on our shoulders. Trusting certainly adds to our peace of mind.

Trust is *allowing* things to happen rather than trying to *make* things happen. That's not always an easy choice. We keep forgetting that our limited experience is not always the last word. We need to allow ourselves to be like little children on monkey bars. We have to let go of one bar before we can grip the next, and that's scary sometimes. But once accomplished, we learn that only the momentum of trust will carry us safely from the past to the future.

There's no lasting happiness without trust. Trust is a part of the magic of life. When people say, "I don't trust," or "I have no trust," they have forgotten how often they trusted that something would not go the way they planned. That indeed is trust. The confusion comes not from the trusting, but, in what is being trusted. In fact, the fear that comes out of trusting that the worst possible thing is about to transpire, demonstrates one of the strongest trusts around.

Trusting that we can make something happen is a show of willfulness, while trusting that we can enjoy whatever happens takes real strength. If we say, "We're absolutely going to sell this house," it's tantamount to saying, "Our will be done." Once we are able to trust our ability to be happy whether or not the house is sold, we begin to discover the real strength of trust. It's this kind of strength that helps make the play of life so much fun. It's the fun of being on a treasure hunt and recognizing that we cannot continue until we've been given the next clue. We will not be given the next clue until we are ready, and since patience has never been one of humankind's most obvious traits, we sometimes have difficulty with this part of the play.

Being

The attachment to who we are is the first one we form and perhaps the last one we let go. Until we can experience that glorious moment of letting go, we can at least begin to let go of the aversions to the person we don't want to be.

Welcome to the world of *being*. In this mode *our number one priority is being good enough. Our first instinct is to compare. Our main consideration is with standards.*

✦ ✦ ✦

Reminder: Setting standards is a common practice in this mode. Whether our standards are raised or lowered makes no difference. The problem exists when we resist what's below our standard. We see it as deficient. Please know that it is not suggested that we accept what we see as deficient; only that we stop seeing it that way. We are the ones setting the standards and creating the resistance. We are the ones projecting the judgment on what we are seeing. It is our judgment, our resistance, not the universe creating the deficiency.

✦ ✦ ✦

As mentioned previously, we all relate to feelings and fighting feelings in different ways. The following true stories are examples of our addictions and aversions. In most cases, the aversions are turned into acceptance, with agreeable results.

Good Enough/Not Good Enough

One of the most amusing, and unfortunately not unusual examples of someone with an aversion to the *not good enough* is Albert. He used to call a lady friend every week or so, saying, "Let's go out and get drunk and *be* somebody." Alcohol allowed him to relax his strict self-judgment and be more relaxed in front of others. Unfortunately, the next morning's hangover was compounded by his guilt over getting drunk, which he saw as being below his standard.

Agnes is a successful therapist in her fifties. She struggled with her aversion to *not good enough* as long as she could remember, and had undergone therapy because of it.

She was an only child and at a young age had convinced herself her parents had wanted a boy. Agnes used this as a pivotal situation to increase her feeling of guilt and her fight with *not good enough*. Her parents never actually told her they wished she had been a boy. However, when one of them suggested she learn the art of self-defense, she convinced herself this was absolute proof her parents would have preferred a child of the masculine gender.

As a result, she tried everything to make it up to them. In high school she conceived the idea that perhaps if she became a doctor, which was her father's profession, she could make up for not being a boy. Fortunately, she never made it. She would not have been a good doctor. Her commitment would never have been to explore the love of medicine. Her commitment would have been to prove that she was *good enough*. Imagine her dilemma had one of her patients died. She would have been destroyed.

It wasn't until many years later that she realized her parents were an excuse for her to act out her resistance to her feelings. They weren't the cause of the feelings at all. Having completed her therapy and given up her resistance, she decided to become a therapist in order to help others overcome their resistance.

The last word on that situation was had by her son. He dropped out of premedical school saying: "Mom, I love you very much, but not enough to be the doctor you wanted to be." It can be very gratifying sometimes when children possess more self-esteem and awareness than their parents.

Perfect/Imperfect

The late Fred Astaire was a shining example of a *being* mode perfectionist. The anecdote about his attending the premiere of his movie *The Story of Vernon and Irene Castle* at Radio City Music Hall tells it all. Midway through one of the dance routines he bolted for a phone. "Get someone out here right away," he told R.K.O. "The film is five frames out of sync." He was able to detect a fraction of a second discrepancy between his movements and the music.

Amy was a gentle, diminutive, and frail-looking actress. Her abilities, however, were enormous. She was one of the more gifted performers in the theater. Her secret dream was to play the role of Lady Macbeth. Since her talent was so extraordinary, her dream inevitably came true. She prepared, as probably no leading lady before her had ever done. She researched the part for over three years and when rehearsal time came, she arrived with all the strength and enthusiasm of the front line of the Denver Broncos.

She also arrived with the standards to match. She insisted that her performance achieve those standards. If it didn't, she would consider the entire project worthless. As the rehearsals progressed, she became more and more disappointed in herself and more and more fatigued. By the time the play opened, although she gave a brilliant performance, she was completely exhausted because of her aversion to anything below her standards. She was also unable to experience the enjoyment of a dream fulfilled.

Dorothy was a top-level editor in a large publishing firm. She lived by the motto, "If it's worth doing, it's worth doing perfectly." By her own admission, she was obsessed with perfection. One day she was asked by a senior vice president to write a memo notifying the entire staff of some changes in policy. "I know I can count on you to write this perfectly," he said.

She worked tirelessly at writing, changing, fixing, and rewriting. When it finally satisfied her as being up to her standard, she handed it to her secretary who looked at Dorothy with dismay. "You sure must have been confused when you wrote this. I can't decipher all those lines and arrows and corrections. You had better stay with me so I can figure it out."

In her aversion to imperfection, Dorothy had become anything but perfect, writing a perfect memo that no one could read.

Success/Failure

Amanda was the first black anchorwoman on a network news program. Though she felt proud and special, she was not truly content. She often said, "What will I do if I lose my job? Then when I walk down the street people won't recognize me or acknowledge me."

Despite her success, her identification with her job would never allow her to see who she really was. So, she constantly relied on other people to reassure her that she was doing well.

Amanda's sister had a different approach to success. She had three boys, ages eighteen, twenty, and twenty-four. "I am the lucky one in the family" she said. "I feel such joy and such love with those kids. They're like good friends. They are happy and secure. I really consider myself a successful mother." It's not unusual for apparently successful people to not appreciate their accomplishment, while those without fame and fortune feel the warm glow of success.

An ancient example of the coexistence of success and failure is a story about an old Chinese farmer, whose ability to accept was the marvel of the town. One day his horse disappeared.

The neighbors commiserated, "Oh, that is too bad!"

"Maybe bad, maybe good," replied the farmer.

A few days later, the horse returned leading four other wild horses with him. The neighbors were just as quick to delight at the farmer's new-found abundance. "Isn't that good fortune?" they cheered.

"Maybe good, maybe bad," was the farmer's reply.

Several weeks later, the farmer's son was trying to tame one of the wild horses. In doing so, he fell and broke his arm.

Again, the neighbors were there with their condolences. "What a shame, such a bad thing had to happen to your son."

Again, the farmer's answer was, "Maybe bad, maybe good."

The following month the army came through the village looking for young men to conscript and send away for a two-year period. Because of his injury, they let the farmer's son stay at home. And so on, and so on. This is proof that we have to include failure on our way to success.

Proper/Improper

Bob was addicted to being diplomatic and had an aversion to rudeness, which he called "bitchiness." He was a twenty-eight-year-old sales manager who had once wanted to be a minister. With his conservative religious background, he understandably avoided the role of the "bitch" like the plague. "Bitches," he said, "hurt people. Nobody likes them. I get terribly upset when I see somebody being bitchy, I just want to leave the room."

Letting go of this limiting reaction seemed to be impossible, but Bob vowed to make friends with his own bitchiness. After two weeks of observing his aversion, he had a breakthrough experience.

He had gone to a Broadway play with a friend and afterward out for coffee with a group of performers. While sitting at the table, one of the young women turned to him and remarked, "I hate New York City. You can't have a decent relationship here. All anyone wants is a one-night stand. Nobody wants to make a real commitment." Then she made the fatal mistake of asking Bob, "Don't you agree?"

He smiled agreeably, being his usual benevolent self, and answered, "I think you can get anything you want in this city. I've seen one night stands and long lasting relationships too. I think the choice is up to the individual."

The woman countered, "I see you like to make clever remarks to stop the conversation." A bitchy remark, indeed.

Bob heard a little voice inside saying, "Now!" The next thing he knew, he heard himself replying, "Well, you see, I live with perceptive people, so it never stops the conversation."

He was stunned by his own reply. A part of his conscious judgment was screaming, "What are you saying?" To no avail, he continued, "And behind that bitch you love to play is someone who is honestly afraid of a real relationship."

In the silence that followed he began to dissolve, wondering how this woman would relate to the outburst so strange and new for him. He wondered if she wouldn't reach across the table and slap him. Instead, she turned to him with a big grin and said, "I like you! Let's talk."

He was honestly astounded. Only later did he understand her somewhat unexpected behavior. She was an actress who was always cast as the sweet, shy ingenue, and she had always wanted to play the villainess. She loved a good exchange of cleverness and wit. When Bob was able to respond freely and let go of the proper behavior, she was genuinely pleased. She was probably impressed by his ability to be both proper and improper with equal ease.

A year later Bob was in a restaurant, and from across the room she waved at him and called his name. She was acknowledging her connection with him, made on a night when he dared to feel and express what he had previously believed could only cause separation.

Powerful/Powerless

Abbey was a young intern who was having a battle letting go of her aversion to feeling powerless. Finally, after many months of trying to make friends with her own powerlessness, she experienced a confirmation of her efforts.

She had just come off a thirty-six-hour shift and was headed home. Before flopping into bed, she decided to spend about thirty minutes in the hospital exercise room. It was early in the morning, very dark, and as she approached the woman's locker room someone grabbed both of her arms from behind. (Incidently, though her attire was otherwise simple, she usually wore enough gold chains to make a dowager look underdressed.) The six-foot-six man behind her turned her around and reached for her gold chains.

At that moment, her old pattern of fighting her powerlessness flooded her being. She closed her eyes and was able to accept and embrace the feeling of powerlessness (not the situation). In a fraction of a second as she relaxed, from the very bowels of her consciousness came a cool sensation of peace. Almost immediately, she heard herself say to her captor, "How dare you! I'm a doctor and I've been up all night taking care of people like you. What do you think you are doing?"

Before she had a chance to react to her own new behavior patterns, the man released her, stepped back, and said, "Gee, lady, I'm sorry. I didn't know you were a doctor. You go ahead and I'll wait out here to be sure you're safe. There are a lot of crazy people around here, you know."

Accepting feeling powerless had allowed the feeling of powerful to follow immediately. Abbey had been mugged twice before and had always frozen and been unable even to yell for help. It was always minutes or even hours later that she had been clear enough to think of all the things she could have said or done. But once she accepted her feeling of powerlessness, the alternatives in the situation become obvious. Her greatest power came when she let go of her need for power.

Keep in mind we are talking about accepting and embracing the *feeling*, not the situation. Once we've done that, the universe somehow shows us what to do next. Acceptance begets more acceptance. Resistance attracts more resistance.

The man in the story, certainly, will never know why he did what he did. It surely wasn't because Abbey said she was a doctor. It wasn't because she yelled at him. It possibly, just possibly, could have been that Abbey had learned what she needed to learn and the universe, God, or her consciousness led her to do exactly what was appropriate.

Some years later, she reported how much more effective she has become as a doctor since she has accepted powerlessness. In the hospital, her colleagues are often frustrated when a patient is dying and there is nothing more for the doctors to do. While the others avoid the dying patient's room because of their own discomfort with feeling powerless, Abbey is able to be present and support the patient. She says, "All I can do is hold the patient's hand and reassure them while they are dying but at least they don't have to die alone." That's the kind of person we'd all like to have around at that time. In accepting that she is powerless to change the situation, she is able to help in one of the most powerful transitions of all.

Secure/Insecure

Betty was a shy, retiring young woman. She claimed she wanted friends more than anything else in the world, that they were her biggest comfort and security. Unfortunately, she was deceiving herself. While Betty claimed she wanted friends, what was even more important was her commitment to avoid anyone who didn't come up to *her* standards. She admitted that when she met new people, she remained very quiet until she was sure that they were the kind of people she wanted to be with. She also admitted that her first impression was not always accurate. Many people she did not like the first time she met them, were really fascinating individuals, and would have been superb friends, if she'd only made friendship more important than her aversion.

One common habit of those of us not able to easily feel secure is our inability to accept compliments. When we are complimented on an article of clothing, how often do we reply, "Oh, this old thing"? What we forget, in our aggressive effort to be humble, is that we are invalidating the person who was saying something nice. The greatest antidote for this universal syndrome are two simple words: "thank you." Try it. It won't hurt, we promise.

Adept/Inept

Bryan Hale was working in the field of textiles for a short while and made numerous calls to interior designers. At that time, he had been dealing with a galloping case of "I have an absolute aversion to ineptitude." Due to the nature of the business, each day he had to make several appointments with people he had never met. This is hardly the easiest way to boost anyone's self-confidence and self-esteem. When he was inept putting all the samples back into his briefcase or forgot someone's name, he tore himself up inside. "How could I be so clumsy?" While graciously smiling and saying goodbye, his thoughts were a jumble of "What's his name? I blew it. I forgot to shake hands with the vice president. What did she just say?"

He began watching his resistance to ineptitude and incapability. After a few weeks he felt he was making great progress. One day he had a textbook-perfect appointment with a woman who specialized in designing stores. He said all the right things, she asked all the proper questions, he gave all the correct answers, and it was great. In short, he had the account in his pocket.

Then, as he triumphantly turned to leave, his coat tail knocked over a small box. In trying to catch it, he stepped back and put his size-thirteen boot heel right through a presentation board. You know the kind—a scale model of the store with tiny trees and people. Startled, he lunged forward, bumping her file cabinet. That was all it took to topple the yellow pages from the top of the file cabinet onto a slanted drafting table. The drawing of a major department store was torn down the center as the yellow pages swooped to the floor, taking two hundred hours of work with it.

In seven seconds he had all but demolished this poor woman's office. He bent over to help clean up the mess when she cried out, "No. You've done enough." At this point, they both looked around and began to laugh. She took Bryan's arm and led him to the elevator saying, "Mr. Hale, why don't you just go home for the rest of the day?" He smiled sheepishly and said, "I can't. I locked myself out this morning."

As he walked down the street, Bryan did an instant replay of what had happened, but this time, something had changed. He seemed to have gone through a sort of final exam on how to handle himself while being totally inept. He had passed with flying colors. He *had* been inept, incapable, clumsy, awkward, and all the other things he had so assiduously avoided.

But because he had learned to watch and not become involved with his resistance, he was unruffled by the incident and shared the story with the rest of his sales office. The freedom of going through what would have been a nightmare before and now was simply an amusing incident, was extraordinary. Furthermore, he never had to worry about being crippled with embarrassment should be ever run into that designer in a restaurant or on the street.

The surprise ending was that this woman gave him the biggest order he received that year. Because he had been inept and it was perfectly all right with him, she was free to call him and admit that *she* was inept when it came to textiles. She admitted fudging her resume to get the job. What a relief to admit it to Bryan, ask his advice, and let him help her out. He explained the various building and fire codes; told her which fabrics to buy, which ones to avoid, and where to go to get everything she needed. His adeptness at feeling inept saved that day and many more to come.

Role Playing

The *being* mode is often one of role playing, since "to be," for most of us, is relating by playing a particular role. The loveliest example comes from a six-year-old who asked his mother if she would play with him.

Half-teasing, the mother replied, "Well, it's been a long time. I'm not sure I know how to play anymore."

Without missing a beat, the boy said, "Mom! Just think for a minute of who you would rather be than anybody else in the world." A bit taken aback, the mother admitted that as a youngster she wanted to be an astronaut. The boy beamed and with a note of great achievement said, "Well, just pretend you are. That's how you play." (That's how we all play.)

One of the best stories about identification with whom we are can be found in an old volume of *Sholam Elecham*. It's a story about the famous Polish Rabbi Zusya. He was asked what he thought God would ask him when he got to heaven. He replied, "I'm sure when I pass through those pearly gates God will not ask me why I was not more like Moses. I'm certain he will ask me why I was not more of Rabbi Zusya."

A Touch of Magic

One of the hardest things for us to deal with is when the work we do is not up to our standard. Therefore, we must be patient with ourselves. We won't be able to get the end results as perfectly or as quickly as we would like. We must give ourselves time—time to fail and to learn a little along the way for it's often through failing that we learn. Without those failures we won't really be accomplishing anything. The most important thing to remember is that one of our most important roles in life is to simply be the watcher, the listener. We just have to be aware of what we are doing, where we are attached and identified. Then a funny thing will happen. For no reason at all, we will start becoming all the things that we really want to be. In all of this, we are never asked to accept only the shadow side of ourselves. We are only asked to bring that part of us that we have kept in the shadows out into the light.

Exercise

Besides watching our feelings and our relationship to who we are, we might be aware of how often we make comparisons. "This day isn't as nice as yesterday." "This job is easier than the last." "He's smarter than she is." "The meal was better last time." Comparisons can't exist without standards to compare. So when we start to compare—and it's astonishing how often we do—we are reminding ourselves of all the standards we've set. Once we recognize how often we compare, we can begin practicing seeing things without comparing them to anything else. We can look at them in the same way a baby might see them, as objects of wonder and discovery.

✦ ✦ ✦

Belief is in the past.
Faith is in the future.
Trust is in the present.

CHAPTER 9

The Art of Having

(Disappointment—The More I Want, the Less I Have)

It's not true that wanting is the root of all pain. Even the Bible admonishes us to ask so we may receive. It's the aversion to not getting what we want that is the culprit. Wanting a bigger, more important job is beneficial to anyone ambitious. Being distraught and unable to accept not getting it, however, is the problem.

Those of us with an aversion in the *having* mode have a bit of a problem with the twins of gratification and disappointment. There can be no hope of gratification without some eventual disappointment. The partnership between gratification and disappointment is pretty much legendary. This doesn't mean disappointment has to be tragic or life-shattering. We have all experienced the disappointment that inevitably follows an attachment to having our heart's desire. If we don't get it or we lose it, we often turn it into a devastating experience. It's all well and good to say, "If you don't want anything, you won't be disappointed." However, that brings up a catch-22. By closing off to the feeling of disappointment, we have also closed ourselves off to gratification, so we don't get our wish either way. Not expecting anything doesn't begin to address the real solution, which is how to enjoy what we have.

Of course, we all want things and we all like to make plans too. Theaters, restaurants, hotels, airlines, barber shops, doctors, to name a few, would all go out of business without plans called "reservations." We expect that if we have tickets for a play, the curtain *will* go up; the plane *will* take off; the doctor *will* keep his or her appointment. However, if we get bent out of shape if a pipe breaks in the Orpheum Theater, the plane is delayed an hour, or the doctor has an emergency, that's the clue we have a little addiction/aversion going on in the field of *having*.

Sports psychologists often give advice such as, "Just keep picturing what you want. Concentrate only on what you want and eventually it will be yours." This kind of obsessive thought pattern may sometimes work, but it also contains a serious flaw. While all of our concentration is riveted on one specific thing, there is no chance for anything else that may be even more desirable to appear. We've virtually locked out anything more desirable the universe may have to offer.

Another very popular addiction in the field of *having* is the need to keep all alternatives open. "I think I want *this* one, but I don't want to miss out on *that* one, or suppose something even better will come along." What follows is the dissatisfaction of being limited to one. "Of course, I could always take *both*." This "salesperson's nightmare" is an all too common occurrence. Advertising doesn't help one iota. We are encouraged to become a nation of collectors. Everything from fine art to McDonald's latest toys are fair game. It's almost impossible to go through a town, no matter how small, without seeing a sign for "collectibles." Collect all twelve, or sixteen, or one hundred is a familiar temptation we hear all the time. The multibillion-dollar Beanie Baby craze is as good an example as any and it isn't just kids who collect them. From trading cards to precious gems, collecting is a practice that allows us to act out, and hopefully become aware of our wanting/ having drive. This way, the avid collector has a perfectly sociable excuse for being a little greedy now and then.

The addiction to what's "out there" is particularly visible in the *having* mode, as long as there is the belief that the experiencer and the experience are separate. "*I* wanna go to the *movies*." "*I* wanna eat dinner *here*." "*I* don't wanna do *that*." "*I* don't want *that* one." The object and the person who wants or doesn't want it are always separated.

We forget the object is just a symbol, and the symbol is only a representation of the feeling and the feeling is within us. We are not separate at all. As *standards* were for the *being* mode, *enough* is the benchmark for the *having* mode. When John D. Rockefeller was asked how much money would be enough, he answered, "Just a little bit more." That is the battle cry of the resister in a *having* mode.

Disappointment

Before we attempt to do away with disappointment, let's take a look at what it really is. Disappointment primarily helps us see where our aversion to missing out, or losing, is even stronger than our addiction to what we want. It's a red light on the road to awareness that forces us to look and see where we are. Where we are is not being able to enjoy what we have. So we go off to the future and put all our energy in expectations rather than into having the present.

Expectations

Expectations play a major role in the *having* mode. For those in this mode, we must remember that whenever we plan something in the future, we stand the chance of getting it or not. Expectations are children of the future and as such, we cannot depend on them. Certainly, it's fun to have something to which we can look forward. Most of us subscribe to the belief that planning is half the fun of the trip. Again, it's not the expectation, but the disappointment of not getting that causes the pain. If the resistance is sufficient and the pain great enough, some people will stop wanting, planning, and expecting altogether. They would rather deprive themselves of all their dreams than have a chance of them being unfulfilled.

Gratification

Falling in love with someone who is married, becoming enamored with people because of their potential rather than who they are at the moment, and being attached to those who state they are not ready for a relationship are common practices for those with the *having* mode out of balance. For those of us with this difficulty, we're fond of saying, "I want it all," but we don't mean it. We want only what we want and only when we want it. We want freedom; we don't want confinement. We want to feel full but never experience emptiness. That's not having it all.

If we had more than we ever dreamed of, we'd still not have the most important thing—the ability to *have*, to appreciate what is already here. We don't need more. We need to learn how to enjoy more. We may claim we want abundance—a huge house, a swollen bank account, or any list of things, but not one of these will give us the experience for which we search. That's why we need more symbols. We often believe that if we have the abundance of symbols, and keep accumulating, sooner or later we'll know gratification. The sad part of this unsatisfying, escalating circle is that it's never-ending.

Greed, by the way, is simply another word for fighting feeling empty, missing out, or not having. Happiness on this planet will be possible only when people understand the difference between abundance and greed. Abundance comes from the celebration and sharing of what we have. Greed is a never-ending cycle of frustration, longing after what we don't have.

It's interesting to note that most people who feel truly abundant, know beyond a shadow of a doubt that there *is* enough to go around.

The Role of Desire

A common distortion of Eastern philosophy is, "To know real pleasure, you must get rid of desire." This is not quite accurate. Desire is the prime motivation for delight. Getting something we want is often the spice of life. The experience of pain doesn't come from wanting, but from the resistance to not getting. The only problem with getting rid of greed, or desire, is that like every other aversion, it's like mercury—the more you step on it, the more it pops up somewhere else. Look at the complaint, "You never give me affection anymore." Has that plea *ever* met with a spontaneous outpouring of love? Chances are it's followed with denial, a counterattack, and most often a withdrawal. The more we try to avoid *not* getting affection, the less we get. Since we can't appreciate what we have, we need more. Lots more.

Opposites Often Attract

Sometimes one aversion seems to attract another. Mrs. C is terrified of *not good enough*. Her husband, Mr. D., resists *confined*. Every time he watches television, switching channels and popping Oreo cookies into an already pudgy face, she sees him as a mirror of her dislike of *not good enough* and tells him to stop. He resists feeling *confined* and sees her request as limiting him. He then eats even more, trying to destroy his feeling of *confinement*, while she tries to eliminate feeling *not good enough*, by continuing to fuss. The battle continues until one falls asleep, leaves the room, or the Oreos are completely consumed. Neither understands why the other is behaving in such a peculiar manner. Their patterns, though sparked by different aversions, are entirely the same.

The same Mrs. C once received a less-than-flattering hair-cut. Her exact comment was, "I look just like a gargoyle." Her haircut became a symbol of her aversion to *not good enough*. Resisting it as she did, she fully expected her husband to make some snide remark. He told her that it didn't matter to him since she'd look beautiful to him anyway.

Mrs. C. was totally flabbergasted. She couldn't understand how he could so readily accept what was so repugnant to her. She couldn't recognize how his fight had nothing to do with *not good enough*. He was accepting and relaxed in that area. However, if she had inadvertently neglected to restock a sup-ply of Oreo cookies, his compassion and understanding would have disappeared on the spot.

Trying to Capture Highs

Throughout history there have been accounts of people at-tempting to capture a "high." Humankind has actually been "turning on" since the beginning of recorded time. It was origi-nally an attempt to find answers. It was not used for fun or what we usually call "gratification." To find answers, primi-tive tribes around the globe ate, drank, and smoked all kinds of natural and concocted substances that added a little aware-ness to their way of life, that broadened and mellowed their perceptions. By using mind-altering substances, the healers and chiefs of the tribes were able to go beyond their attachment, their addictions and their aversions, to where all the answers lie. Today the drug scene is quite different. The crack addict's revelation that the aversion to the pain of "coming down" was more important than the high told the story.

Once more, it's not the addiction but the aversion that guides our choice. Especially in this "longing and loathing" area, it's avoiding the disappointment, more than fulfilling the gratifications, that takes over. To be stuck in the loathing is to say, "I want gratification, even though I wouldn't know how to experience it if it sat on my lap."

In the last analysis we must remember that disappointment may be seen as not getting what we want, but in reality, it's not being able to see what we have. Once we are able to enjoy *that*, we truly will have it all.

Our attachment to our possessions and our toys is a strong one. Until we can honestly mimic the great Greek philosopher Kosanzakus by saying, "I want nothing. I have nothing. I am free," we will probably have a few addictions and aversions here.

Welcome to the world of *having*. In this mode *our number one priority is having enough. Our first instinct is to protect what we have. Our first consideration is with quantity.*

✦ ✦ ✦

Reminder: Setting expectations is particularly prevalent in this mode. While we are usually satisfied when things meet our expectations, we're usually dissatisfied when they don't. To be able to enjoy whatever happens, whether it meets our expectations or not, is real freedom. Since we're the ones who set up and fight our expectations not being met, it stands to reason that we're the ones to drop the fight, and participate joyously in what is going on.

✦ ✦ ✦

The following true stories deal not only with having things but having experiences. Experiences are vitally important to those of us in a *having* mode. The expectation of an experience, is possibly one of the most crucial things in having it our way. In fact, one extremely bright, sensitive, young woman, claimed that her most painful times in life were when she perceived someone had stolen her experience—and she was serious. If, for example, she had decided to go somewhere and circumstances dictated she go somewhere else, she would say that the person responsible for the change in plans had stolen her experience. She would not accept the new one or be open to any that were not part of her expectation. With this aversion, she was seldom able to enjoy herself. The thought of impending disappointment and the universe not meeting her expectations was always in the back of her mind.

Abundant/Lacking

Carl had been talking about cleaning out his closets for almost two years. He began only when they were practically overflowing. The contents eventually spilled over into the living room and finding a place to sit soon became difficult. He was constantly apologizing for the clutter. Finally he became so embarrassed he refused to invite anyone into his home. If a friend stopped by or a delivery was made, he would peer through the peephole and send the visitor away.

One day a close friend came to Carl's rescue. She was an interior designer and offered to help Carl with his closet dilemma by making new shelves and rearranging space—anything that would help Carl's storage challenge. She surveyed the situation and came up with a full set of plans and some practical solutions. The entire process would take three hours, she said. Carl agreed to proceed with the project as soon as he could set aside the time. Four months later nothing had been done. When Carl was questioned about why it was taking him so long to find three hours for a long-overdue project, his reply was, "It's not three hours, it's four and a half. I can't tackle a big project like that without a big dinner first. I need a reward so I can face what has to be done."

One of the best stories about someone in a *having* addiction comes from an old Sufi legend: There was once a stonecutter who was dissatisfied with himself and with his position and role in life. One day, he passed a wealthy merchant's house and, through the open gateway, saw many fine possessions and important visitors.

"How powerful that merchant must be!" thought the stone-cutter. He became very envious, and wished that he could be the merchant, and not a mere stonecutter. To his great surprise, he suddenly became the merchant, enjoying more luxuries and power than he had ever dreamed of, envied and detested by those less wealthy than himself. But soon a high official passed by, carried in a sedan chair, accompanied by attendants, and escorted by soldiers beating gongs. Everyone, no matter how wealthy, had to bow low before the procession.

"How powerful that official is!" he thought. "I wish that I could be a high official!" He then became the high official, carried everywhere in his embroidered sedan chair, feared and hated by the people all around who had to bow down before him as he passed. It was a hot summer day, and the official felt very uncomfortable in the sticky sedan chair. He looked up at the sun. It shone proudly in the sky, unaffected by his presence.

"How powerful the sun is!" he thought. "I wish that I could be the sun!" He then became the sun, shining fiercely down on everyone, scorching the fields, cursed by the farmers and laborers. But a huge black cloud moved between him and the earth so his light could no longer shine on everything below.

"How powerful that storm cloud is!" he thought. "I wish that I could be a cloud!" He then became the cloud, causing rain to flood the fields and villages and was shouted at by everyone. But soon he found that he was being pushed away by some great force and realized it was the wind.

"How powerful it is!" he thought. "I wish that I could be the wind!" He then became the wind, blowing tiles off the roofs of houses, uprooting trees, hated and feared by all below him. But after a while, he ran up against something that would not move, no matter how forcefully he blew against it—a huge, towering stone.

"How powerful that stone is!" he thought. "I wish that I could be a stone!" Then he became the stone, more powerful than anything else on earth. But as he stood there, he heard the sound of a hammer pounding a chisel into the solid rock and felt himself being changed.

"What could be more powerful than I, the stone?" he thought. He looked down and saw far below him the figure of a stonecutter.

Empty/Full

Catherine, a talented, charming young woman had not been able to find a steady boyfriend despite having spent every minute of the last ten years looking. All she ever attracted were men who were unavailable—married men terrified of commitment, boys looking for a mother, older men only looking to recapture their youth. When an eligible man did appear on the horizon, her aversion to feeling empty charged forth as neediness. She came on like gangbusters, needy and suffocating. The poor man would shrink away in self-defense. She was not aware that desperation is the last gambit for seduction and that "aloneness" can be most enjoyable. "Loneliness," on the other hand, is simply fighting being by oneself.

Having/Missing Out

David was a true social butterfly. He loved parties, dancing, theater, opera, and lectures. A social event was a real treat for him. It was also one of his real challenges. Because his main aversion in life was to giving anything up, the universe mirrored his commitment, and gave him an abundance of I-have-to-give-something-up situations. Every time there was a special occasion for David, there seemed to be another equally important occasion at the same time. He was seldom able to make plans for something without something else being in conflict. A typical evening involved a concert and a party. The cocktail party would start at 7:00 P.M. and the concert at 8:00 P.M. David would usually plan to attend the cocktail party first, stay until 8:30, and arrive at the concert late. Invariably the party wouldn't start getting interesting until just before he planned to leave for the concert, and by the time he arrived, the thing he most wanted to hear had already been played.

Once we can remember that if we are willing to give up one thing, we will be able to completely enjoy the other, we'll have a much better time. The ability to spend more energy enjoying what we have, rather than longing after what we don't, is one of the finest talents that we can acquire. Otherwise, we'll never be pleased, because no matter what we have, our attention will be on what is missing.

Structured/Unstructured

Structure is a diabolical creation. It can be a symbol of both freedom and confinement. For some people it's a godsend. For others, it's a curse. The problem with structure is that we need it, and yet, we sometimes overuse it. Words are one example. We need words to communicate, however, we also forget that they are not the object that we are describing. We need to know the word menu to select a meal, but if we believe that the menu is the meal, we've lost touch with reality.

A trio of three friends used structure as diversely as we might imagine. Carla needed structure desperately. She would rush home from the office, making absolutely sure she arrived at the exact prescribed moment, even though there wasn't a soul there. She set her expectations and nothing—the unexpected visit of a long lost friend, the sudden need for a board meeting, the appearance of an office crisis—would deter her from arriving home at exactly 5:55 P.M. When asked why, she replied that staying within that structure gave her a feeling of protection that nothing else seemed to do.

Caren had no use for structure whatsoever. She avoided it at all costs. She would take twice as long to do something that requires even a modicum of form or configuration. Her reason was that she used structure as a symbol of someone telling her what to do. She found it limiting.

Connie used structure to meet expectations. She said that when she followed a particular pattern, she usually got what she wanted. It served as a true physical aid.

Here we have structure as a watchdog, an enemy, and a friend. Which one is it? All of them. None of them. It depends on how we wish to see it. The same applies to the entire world around us. Whatever we choose to make us happy or make us crazy is strictly our choice. The structure really doesn't care. Like all symbols, it's willing to play any role we want it to play.

Tardiness is another attempt to manipulate structure. Some people are late in order to be noticed. Others feel that the structure of time is an imposition and uncreative, and will therefore, not obey it. Still others use time as an object of control. "You can't leave until I'm good and ready, and there's nothing you can do about it." All tardiness has to do with manipulation of other people, so the best the rest of us can do is go on about our lives with our own schedules.

Limitless/Limited

One of the saddest roles to perceive is the person who is bored and resigned to being limited. There's no point in attempting to interest someone who has resigned from having fun. One who has chosen to be bored has made a very conscious decision. This role is particularly prevalent with teenagers. The cause has been debated in psychologists' quarters, schools, and homes throughout the country. The fact that it's "cool" is the closest anyone has yet been able to get. Perhaps since the process of growing up is such an exciting one, there is, indeed, a part of the process that must be dull. Judging enthusiasm to be "not cool" is a cool way to create boredom. Boredom is often considered to be our refusal to venture deeper into any subject or situation. Since there is a decision not to have fun, the obvious alternative would seem to be to do something useful and something where fun is not expected—like doing the dishes, homework, vacuuming the rug, or washing the car. After a few suggestions of this nature, many teenagers have been known to change their attitude entirely and even find a bit of interest in what they have chosen to do instead.

Gain/Loss

Of all the lessons in not *having*, one of the biggest any of us has to learn is the ability to accept the feeling of loss. It's a lesson that we must all face. No one is exempt from it. Yet, we all try to avoid it. Protection against loss has fostered one of the largest businesses in the country—insurance. Still, trying to protect against it is like living life through an emotional prophylactic. Attempting to avoid loss is also like reaching out to life with a closed fist. Unless we're willing to accept that loss is always followed by gain, we will continue to block the loss and the gain as well.

The disappointment we experience when faced with loss is something to which everyone can relate. Yet, we seldom stop to think that the loss of one thing can open the door to the gain of something else. Julie Andrews' award-winning role in *The Sound of Music* more than made up for her loss of the movie role in *My Fair Lady*. It's often our constant resistance to the feeling of loss that doesn't allow us to see the myriad possibilities and alternatives presenting themselves.

Chris and Donna had been going together all through high school and planned to get married as soon as Chris finished college. They were the school's golden couple, though they were hardly a personality match. Donna was bright and ambitious, with a love of learning and discovery. Chris' interests were mostly limited to parties and football. It was no surprise that he was hardly a shining light at college. It was also no surprise that shortly after he arrived at school he found a new girlfriend whose main priority matched his. The inevitable happened. Faithful Donna, who had promised to wait, suffered enormously. She was truly crushed by the loss of what she expected to be her lifetime partner. It was almost a year before she even considered dating again. Then, one of the most attractive, eligible bachelors in town dated her, wined her, dined her, and a year later married her.

While this may sound like a piece of "Pollyanna prose," it's a true story and an honest example of what can happen when we let go of grieving over loss, and wake up to all that we can gain.

Fighting the feeling of the disappointment of loss, can lead to bizarre behavior patterns. Dina was such a fighter. Her resistance to loss began when her brother died. She was inconsolable and began to retire from life. She stopped talking to her friends. She refused to see people, even those who were like family to her. Finally, her parents sought medical help for her. A brilliant and compassionate doctor cared for her for almost two years.

After that time, she joined the world again. She got a job, made new friends, did some traveling, and for a short time, even had a serious relationship with a young man. One thing she still refused to do, however, was acquire personal belongings. She had traded her resistance to losing a person to one of losing things. People were no longer her symbol of loss—*things* took their place. She had such an aversion to the possible loss of possessions, that she would not buy or accept anything that didn't fit into her small backpack. If someone gave her a present and it didn't fit easily into her container of worldly goods, she'd pass it on to someone else, saying that she was recycling. Mind you, she was not living in a campground. She was living in a rented room in the city. She learned to function, to cope, but never to truly enjoy the abundance that life can provide.

Providing/Protecting

Dan used to have an awful time sending gifts to his demanding mother. He would put it off as long as possible and then the flowers or presents would arrive the day after Easter, the week after Christmas, or an hour after her birthday party ended. He admitted he was avoiding "having to." He loved his mother and enjoyed providing for her; he was just not able to deal with the idea that he had to provide on schedule. (More structure.) Being a resourceful young man, he came up with the idea of sending his mother presents on "Happy Thursday in August" or on "Just for Nothing" day or "Because I Love You." He hasn't sent her a Mother's Day gift in ten years, but there's not been one complaint.

There *are* ways to pamper our aversions to our less-than-favorite feelings. The difficulty with that is that sooner or later, we're going to have to face them, and the longer we put it off, the harder it becomes. It's true that most people spend a lifetime attempting to avoid what they don't want, and never develop a talent for enjoying what they have. It's the old story of running from the goblins, rather than to the angels. When our life is full of goblin tracks, we can be certain it's time to turn our attention in the other direction. Accepting feelings for the joy and the pleasure we can derive from them, is simply *that*, and not a tricky way of getting rid of what we haven't been able to enjoy. If we hold on to a relationship that's not working, and pretend that everything's fine, our life won't work. Once we begin to recognize that "losing and having" is an ongoing game, and that we are all conscripted, we will have picked up at least part of the message. Life is a "turned on experience." If that's not obvious, it's because our thumb is on the "off" button.

The big trick in the *having* mode is practicing how to really have. It's not something to be practiced now and then, or once in a while. It needs to be practiced all the time—every day—as often as possible. The extraordinary result is that the more we practice, the more we enjoy. The more we enjoy, the more we appreciate. The more we appreciate, the more loving we become, a habit that will be with us forever. There is no such thing as loss as we once knew it, for whatever is loved cannot die. We have so much. We will never use up one-tenth of what we have. Let us rejoice and celebrate what is, lest we live only for our longing for what is not.

✦ ✦ ✦

Nothing is missing
Everything we want is here.
We just don't see it.

CHAPTER 10

The Art of Doing

(Discouragement—Where's the Mona Lisa? I'm Double-Parked)

"Keep your eye on the goal" has been the slogan of big business for as long as most of us can remember. The end result has justified the means more times than not. Task-oriented, goal-oriented, result-oriented people have been our role models in almost every field. Consequently, in the *doing* mode, the main effort is not around doing but around getting things done.

This presents a small problem. The addiction to achievement does not include the pleasure of achieving! Once again, the addiction to achieving is fueled by our aversion to not having achieved, as convoluted as that may sound. Since we are running from the goblin of nonachievement, our main concern in the *doing* mode is not to get things done properly or the pleasure of the doing, but just to get them done. In resistance, when we are not able to complete a task, we tend to become discouraged. Discouragement is the symptom of not being able to achieve something. It thrives in the area of goal-setting. It is hovering any time we are addicted to making things happen. Discouragement, when carried to an extreme, can become futility. It is often accompanied by the cries of "This will never be finished." "I'll never lose weight." "People will always put their priorities ahead of mine." We all have our priorities, of course. What we fail to recognize when we're in resistance is that our priorities are not necessarily universal priorities.

One of the most difficult things to do, when we're addicted to *making something happen*, is simply *letting it happen*, but that's just what we must learn to do if we expect to find even a semblance of balance in this mode. We must realize that true joy cannot be achieved, only uncovered. As with sex, we cannot force an orgasm, we have to let it happen. We're adept at being able to manipulate a situation. Then do we have to learn how to manipulate ourselves out of manipulating? Unfortunately, we can't do it. We have to simply observe, watch, witness, and see just what we're doing, without any commitment to changing it, and that's a monumental task for someone addicted to getting things done.

Why the necessity for what looks like inactivity? First of all, it's not inactivity. It's a process that requires the gentle art of listening, which means creating a plan, moving on it, and then waiting to see how it unfolds before moving again. While trying to make something happen, we are incapable of experiencing what's actually happening. Without experiencing what's happening, we won't be aware of what we need to do next. It's as though we were saying, "My will be done—regardless." That eliminates the feedback we need for a possible revision of our original plan. When we remember how few plans ever come to fruition without a few changes, we can see how unsuccessful forcing any plan can be.

Unfortunately, many of us have accepted the belief that if we don't continue to push and struggle, we will lose our motivation and become lazy. We have been told that laziness and lack of motivation are synonymous. Nothing could be further from the truth. Laziness is highly motivated. It is fired by the motivation of fighting, or resisting doing something. Laziness is not relaxing and enjoying doing nothing. Relaxing reduces stress. Fighting anything, including doing nothing, produces stress, which is why people who dislike their jobs are stressed. People who love their jobs seldom are. This is why some motivational training is unsuccessful. Motivation built on avoidance doesn't work. To tell a sales unit they must outsell their competitors or they'll be losers is counterproductive. Yet, it's astonishing the number of seminars that are built on this useless technique.

Enthusiasm

The partner or the twin of *discouragement* is *enthusiasm.* The honest enthusiasm shown in projects is often the very thing that completes them and makes them outstanding. The ability to truly enjoy whatever it is we've chosen as a purpose is probably the most important thing in the entire purpose—just as trusting who we are and being gratified with what we have are essential for our well-being. In the same way, being enthusiastic about what we're doing, is also essential for our well-being. Using our energy to judge what is purposeless and what is meaningless only gets in the way of enthusiasm.

An addiction to doing only what is judged purposeful is not uncommon in the *doing* mode. The need for everything to have *real meaning* is so important to some of us we even make a purpose out of doing nothing.

Ethel was such an addict. She was seated on her large terrace one day, sunning herself, when she got up from her chair and bolted inside. Her friend, mildly concerned about Ethel's rush to go indoors, asked if anything was the matter. She was amused to hear the reply, "I have to go in and get some work done so I can come out here and relax." With an addiction/aversion in the *doing* mode, purpose must be completed before a reward can be contemplated.

The Goal Is All

With all the emphasis in today's society on achievement and accomplishment, we often forget that achievements and accomplishments are symbols too. Goals and purposes are only places to stay overnight on our way. We can't live there. When we resist nonaccomplishment, we are playing with a double-edged sword. Accomplishment inevitably leads to completion, and if we have to always be accomplishing a goal, once there's a completion, we panic because there's nothing more to do. We have to find something else with a purpose. Is there a better treadmill syndrome, a more defeating scenario? Discouragement at not being able to complete a project is surpassed only by not having any project to complete. To a purposeless avoider, the only words worse than, "It's not done," are "There's nothing more to do." The ultimate purposeless fighter is the person who in the midst of utter joy says, "Boy, I feel wonderful and lighthearted. But I can't stay like this all day! I have to come down and accomplish something meaningful."

Welcome to the world of *doing*. In this mode o*ur number one priority is our purpose. Our first instinct is to complete. Our first consideration is what's meaningful.*

✦ ✦ ✦

Reminder: Goals and end results are the hallmark of this mode. However, being able to delight in the process along the way, whether our goal is achieved or not, is the most satisfying purpose to which we can aspire. After all, no matter how important or how urgent the end result may seem, at the very best it is a temporary accomplishment.

✦ ✦ ✦

Accomplished/Unaccomplished

Accomplishing is not necessarily limited to large projects. The simple act of finishing a meal or closing a conversation is important to us when we're in a *doing* mode. The secret to enjoying getting things done and getting them done easily, is in bringing our attention to each detail along the way.

Edgar had a severe case of the flu. Unfortunately, he had an appointment that was virtually impossible to cancel or postpone. As he lay in bed, his head swimming at the prospect of all that had to be done to get to his appointment, he remembered this secret. Edgar was a dedicated man and would do anything to arrive at his end result. He started slowly asking himself, "Can I *just* pull back the covers? Now, can I *just* swing my legs over the side of the bed? Can I stand up? Can I walk to the shower? Now, can I *just* slip out of my pajamas? Can I get *into* the shower?" He kept this up until the entire project was completed successfully. It may sound as though he carried "one thing at a time" to an extreme, but some situations call for extreme focusing and that's what he did. He let go of any end result and committed to taking one tiny step at a time—being in the moment at all times.

Being in the moment is the greatest antidote for the addiction to accomplishment or the aversion to not accomplishing. The polarity of Edgar's behavior was a young man in a New York taxi late one evening. The driver noted he was bouncing from one side of the seat to another. He then put down one of the jump seats and sat on it. After a few moments, he replaced the jump seat and slid back to the back seat. Shortly, he put down the other jump seat and did the whole procedure all over again. After the third run through all of this frenetic behavior, the driver asked, with usual New York taxi driver compassion, "Hey, mister, why don't you just sit back and relax?"

The passenger replied, "I can't. I've got to get home and get to sleep. I have a big project to start tomorrow."

Productive/Unproductive

Jim and June had been married for over twenty years. They were considered "the golden couple" in that no one ever heard either of them utter a harsh word. They seldom disagreed and never argued or had what could be considered a fight. Their number one priority was the same but their aversions were quite different. He had a strong aversion to missing out, while her resistance to incompletion was legend. The difference became quite apparent when they began writing a book together. June had a strong addiction to accomplishing things, and particularly to finishing them, while Jim craved alternatives.

Every evening when June had "finished" her first draft, she would heave a sigh of joy at having completed the task. Jim would then burst with excitement about how to write it another way or add something to it. Wanting to avoid incompletion, June would lapse into discouragement at never being able to see any of her work completed. Jim would be disappointed by not being able to change and make "improvements." Until they both began to watch their addiction/aversion pattern, and make writing the book a more important commitment than what they wanted to avoid, the book went nowhere. Once they did, the book got written, published, and rewritten into what you are reading here.

We are so often anxious to complete—to finish—as though the whole purpose of life were to complete it. Nothing is ever complete. Everything is a process. While we can complete one part of the process, there is always more to be done.

Let's look at housework. Floors are never cleaned permanently. There will always be dishes to be washed. A relationship, at least a good one, is never finished. A person is never a finished product. One of the more insightful bumper stickers reads, "Be patient. God isn't finished with me yet." We are all processes. Everyone is a living, breathing project under construction, and every once in a while our scaffolding shows.

Purposeful/Purposeless

The thing we want to achieve is not necessarily something others will applaud. It can, in fact, be something others consider less than desirable. Gena had such an achievement. She was what some people would label an alcoholic. She never went on binges, and she never drank on the job. She did, however, manage to consume a fifth of Jack Daniels each day. On those rare occasions of a party or a vacation, she drank as though prohibition was just around the corner. Although she had never asked herself why she drank, one day she heard herself say, "I'm going to build myself a drink." She realized that drinking was her only purpose and commitment when she wasn't working. She couldn't be without something to do, so she worked at drinking. She gave it her all, just like any other job, and she achieved her purpose.

What About the Old Folks?

One of the greatest apprehensions many of us have about aging is that we won't be able to achieve the same things anymore. The truth is that we won't. We can, however, learn to achieve something else—if we're open to change. Our resistance to letting go of old achievements to acquire new ones, can leave us pathetically disillusioned and discouraged. We forget that the people who can play a great game of golf at age eighty or a smashing game of tennis at sixty-five, do so because they are interested in life. They aren't interested in life because they can still play golf or tennis.

When we see our loved ones staring off into space, we tend to judge that their lack of attention is sad. Sometimes it is. Sometimes their fight with being out of mental control is disheartening. Sometimes, though, they are off in a world of fantasy that's far more pleasant and entertaining than what we're doing at the moment. "But it's fantasy" we say. It certainly is, but how much of our lives that we call reality is really fantasy. Plans are fantasies. Goals are fantasies, and most of all, our opinions and our concepts are fantasies. If, as we grow older, we could put the emphasis on enjoying what we *are doing*, rather than trying to retain or recapture the fantasy of what we used to do, we would experience a much happier, freer, and perhaps an even more productive old age.

Mr. Wong

The obsession with achieving purposeful things is the point of a delightful story by sixth-century philosopher Chuang Tzu.

Mr. Wong was one of the richest men along the Yang Tse River. His boats sailed by daily, laden with produce and potential profit. He had many factories, all of which were run by his five healthy and intelligent sons. His family life was equally successful, though not serene. He was plagued by doubt and despair. Nothing he did truly satisfied him. Each day had to present him with something meaningful or he considered it a waste of time. So great was his discomfort that he sought the advice of the wise man of the village.

His splendid coach arrived at the wise man's house early one morning. The wise man greeted Mr. Wong graciously, listened to his plight and agreed to help the troubled merchant. First, he sent the coach away and then bid Mr. Wong to sit and have some tea. Although this kind of activity was not Mr. Wong's usual practice, he tolerated what he considered a waste of time in order to solve his problem.

Several hours later, the wise man and an impatient Mr. Wong left the house and walked slowly into town. There they met a kind, gentle old man, Mr. Chin. He was the antithesis of Mr. Wong. Mr. Chin moved slowly and deliberately, noticing everything along the path. He was not only observant, he took time to enjoy everything. Nothing escaped his genuine interest. Above all, he was the happiest, most contented man Mr. Wong had ever seen.

"How does he achieve such a state of serenity?" Mr. Wong asked the wise man.

"By finding purpose in all that is presented to him. Nothing is of great urgency, yet nothing is overlooked," the wise man replied.

"He must be a very wealthy man not to have to concern himself with the insistent demands of life," Mr. Wong said.

"Quite the opposite," the wise man assured him. "Mr. Chin lives on a very modest pension. He spends his time shopping for inexpensive food and enjoys meeting and talking with the myriad of friends he has made over the years. Occasionally, he will find a particularly beautiful flower in the marketplace and he will purchase it. He will take it home and share it with a friend, along with a pot of tea. They will turn this into a very joyous and auspicious occasion."

"Has he never accomplished anything?" Mr. Wong asked.

"He has written several well-respected, widely read books of poetry. However, Mr. Chin believes that living a joyous life, rich in experience, is his greatest achievement."

"Then he does know the anguish and pressure of priorities. He must have felt pain when the muse of creativity was unreachable, when the words wouldn't come," said Mr. Wong.

On hearing the conversation, Mr. Chin turned to the two men and smiled. "I have allowed the muses to work in their own time. I know the exhilaration and the excitement of being led to an idea. When that happens, I work steadily with abounding joy. When I am no longer in touch with my creativity, I stop. I cannot force what does not come easily."

"But you can't be lazy and be a successful writer."

"I'm not lazy. I have come to know the difference between demanding that the muse lead me and allowing myself to be led. When I'm open to experience purpose in every step, I am less anxious about the actual accomplishment of the task. Now I use every step to experience that feeling of accomplishment. Each activity is but a reminder of my experience—never a substitute."

The wise man nodded to Mr. Chin. They bowed to one another and departed, leaving a very puzzled, but hopefully, a more enlightened Mr. Wong.

Be Here Now

While not all of us have the luxury of waiting for the whim of the muse, we do have the opportunity and time to focus and enjoy the moment, every moment. The ability to be "here and now" is the most successful way to achieve anything.

There is a dilemma when we are faced with addictions and aversions in the *doing* mode. We need the exhilaration of having accomplished with a guarantee that there will always be more to do. Getting things done and having things to do at the same time is pretty paradoxical, when you stop to think about it. That's quite a bit to ask. Especially when we find so little joy in the only time we truly have—the eternal now. Once we can shift our boundless energy from the end result of a project, to being more aware of everything around us, our path will become less demanding, and much more interesting. When we get stuck in the *doing* mode, we would do well to remember that we don't have to achieve to deserve joy and peace! Simply enjoying and being peaceful is probably the greatest achievement of all.

Exercise

One of the easiest ways to catch ourselves rushing to complete something and not being in the moment with the project is—whenever we're so engrossed in what we're doing that we forget to enjoy the process. *Stop* and count to ten. If this feels like an interruption or an annoyance, we can be pretty certain that we're working from a place where we're not open to anything that might make the project better and more fun.

✦ ✦ ✦

When purpose has been
used to avoid purposeless,
nothing has been gained.

✦ ✦ ✦

CHAPTER 11

The Art of Connecting
(*Anger—It's All Your Fault Anyway*)

More than any of the other three modes, the *connecting* mode has to do with "out there." It stands to reason that if we're looking for something, or someone with whom to connect, it must be "out there," separate from us. This is the very basis of *connection/disconnection:* "There is *us* and there is *the world around us,*" or what Alan Watts calls "outside our bag of skin." We're like a little wave insisting we're not part of the ocean and wanting to make a connection.

Relationships are a perfect example of "them" and "us," which we might call "subject" and "object." "I" am the subject and "he" is the object, or vice-versa. It doesn't matter. Either way, "he" and "I" are separate. That way we can either connect or disconnect; and if I have an aversion to disconnection, and he disconnects first, "he" is wrong. "He" is to blame and "I" am angry. In the *connecting* mode, the clue to our aversion is *anger* and we usually need to be angry with someone "out there." This is not to say that we never become angry with ourselves, or blame ourselves, but most of the time, anger is directed outward not inward. Surely we can be afraid of something "out there" or disappointed in not getting something "out there" or even discouraged in not accomplishing something "out there." However, "out there" looms most formidable when it's combined with fault and blame. Since *anger* takes the form of an outward thrust, we must find something "out there" to thrust against. Even when we're angry at a part of ourselves, we've separated that part from the rest as the target of our anger.

Where does this anger come from? The seat of most *anger* lies in the belief that someone has said or done something that we consider to be *wrong*. This may sound overly simplistic, but sometimes simple truth can be the most accurate.

The wrongdoing can be found in many different areas. One is in doing something without our consent, or even our knowledge. Often it is the sin of *disconnecting*. Betrayal and abandonment are both in this category since they arise from someone disconnecting without our permission. The person just did what he or she did—disconnect. *We* saw it as abandonment, betrayal, or desertion because we have an aversion to disconnection.

The aversion to being betrayed and disconnected is certainly one of the most universal. Christ's second-to-last words on the cross were, *"Eli Eli Ala Sabach Tani.* My God. My God, why hast thou forsaken me?" If even Jesus had a problem with this addiction/aversion, we shouldn't be too surprised at its presence. He did, of course, finally accept, saying, "Father into thy hands do I commit My spirit."

Another area of wrongdoing, which is even more common, is when someone makes a direct attack on who we believe we really are. It's an affront to our very self-image, our identification, our separate, individual self—our ego. The only thing that can anger people faster than telling them they're wrong is telling them they are someone or something other than who they believe themselves to be. We all create our own sacred identity, and when someone refuses to respect and accept that specific image, we look on their behavior as sacrilegious. Attempting to extricate someone from their carefully chiseled self-image will cause major discomfort, to say the least.

As long as we believe we are separate from others and as long as we resist being told we're incorrect, overlooked, or not respected, we will respond with *anger*. Then we will have to find someone "out there" to be responsible for our resistance. Being angry at a person, a symbol, is far more satisfying than being angry at our own feeling. With a symbol we have the delicious pleasure of looking forward to destroying it, punishing it, getting even with it, or taking revenge on it. None of the above are possible with a feeling and it's the feeling we're really resisting. We won't be upset when we see a child being punished unless we believe he or she is being victimized, invalidated, or in some way wrongly treated. We don't blame the mother, unless we use her as a symbol of our resistance to a feeling.

Switching from blaming the symbol (the mother) to recognizing the aversion to the feeling it represents (victimized) is not always easy. However, recognizing our aversion is one way to finally connect with our feelings.

If someone behind us in the elevator jabs us in the ribs, chances are *anger* will happen. We'll fight feeling disrespected or violated. However, if we discover that the person is blind, we'll soon choose another feeling. Why? It was the same person who did the same thing. We chose to be angry and fight feeling a lack of respect. Now we look silly, since there was no lack of respect. But suppose there was? Why did we have to be angry? Because we wanted to act out a resistance to violation, so we jumped at this chance. Only when we're aware of the entire process, and recognize our trigger-happy response to a possible insult, will we find it amusing.

Road rage is the same story line. We don't know if the "stupid idiot" who cut us off was rushing to an emergency. However, because of our aversion to a feeling of invalidation, we're sometimes willing to put both of our lives in jeopardy.

Let's face it. If someone invalidates us, it's easier to direct our anger toward that person and imagine all sorts of retribution, than to face our own resistance to feeling invalidated.

Invalidation—Beyond the Ego

Invalidation is one of those feelings we most love to fight. More of us have an aversion to invalidation than possibly any other feeling in the *connecting* mode. It's a very amorphous word and covers a great deal of feeling territory.

What does it actually mean? Invalidation has at least three forms. It may first suggest "making wrong." Whenever someone says to us, "No that's not it," or "That's not what happened," they have invalidated us. Second, if they totally ignore us, they're invalidating us—pretending we don't exist. The third form of invalidation we have mentioned previously. It is being told we are somebody or are doing or feeling something that is not our experience. Telling a child, "Stop crying. It doesn't hurt," is one common example. How do we know how much it hurts? Not allowing people to have their experience, telling them what they should be feeling when that's not what they're feeling at all, is invalidation—big time. For those of us who resist it—the resistance hurts a lot! There is, of course, an alternate response to resisting the feeling of invalidation.

As we said, invalidation is not the feeling most people choose as their favorite experience. However, when accepted with compassion, invalidation is one of the most rewarding, transcending forms of autonomy. Meditating, people-watching, disappearing into an event, being consumed by a project, losing ourselves in a breathtaking view are all forms of invalidation, of going beyond *connecting*, into celebrating oneness. They are all examples of how we can go beyond our individual separate identity, and become something greater. Invalidation is simply going beyond our ego—that specific part of self that we believe is separate from everything else. Validation and connection define exactly who we think we are, while invalidation allows us to be *less* or *more* than we think we can be.

Validation is limitation. "I am only this." "I am *not* that." Invalidation includes all that which exists beyond the limitation. When we are able to do something beyond our wildest dreams, we have invalidated ourselves. Even when someone invalidates us by saying we are something we don't believe we are, they have just added to our totality. They have given a new facet to our being. Whether we like it or not, that's how they see us. To them, that's who we are.

✦ ✦ ✦

Remember: Nobody likes us or dislikes us. They only like the image they've created to fit their own scenario. We have no control over that. What we can decide for ourselves is how much willingness we can show in our own response, or how much we willfully demand that people see us in exactly the image we have prescribed.

✦ ✦ ✦

Validation sets boundaries. That brings up our need to connect. Invalidation exists beyond all boundaries. It cannot be limited. When we feel as though someone is invading our space, we might remember that if we don't claim space as ours, no one can invade it. The moment we construct walls and boundaries, someone will be there to knock them down. The instant we are willing to relinquish our independent identity— our separateness, our ego—we automatically fuse with the universe. Acceptance is where a separate self, a personal identity is no longer of value. It is where willingness allows us to be anything and everything we choose to be.

Denying

Denying is a way of invalidating what we have been told as the truth. Rather than trying to destroy it, we just pretend it doesn't exist. We would rather deny the situation than *connect* with a feeling to which we have an aversion. The mother who denies her son's illegal activities, the lover who denies his infidelity, the business woman who denies her unfair business practices, the Alzheimer's patient who denies his failing intellectual capacity, are all identified with one specific aspect of their personality and won't connect with any other.

You Are Wrong and I Can Prove it

Many symbols can be both seductive and validating. Some of the best convincers and validators are statistics, facts and figures, logic and proof. Statistics are the ultimate weapon for those of us avoiding invalidation. They seduce us into believing that the only real world is their world. When we're angry, we often use facts and figures. They serve to persuade us that we are right and the other person is wrong. Facts and figures are used, particularly, by people who see themselves as an ultimate authority. There's one in every group. He or she claims to have been everywhere and done everything. We've all known people who, no matter what the subject, they have to have the last word. Why? Usually, because they have a difficult time connecting with other people—deeply connecting—so they connect instead with information and facts and figures. That way, since most of them have a strong aversion to feeling disconnected, they're not stranded "out there" alone. They have their statistics to keep them warm. In the movie *Rain Man,* the character Dustin Hoffman played was the quintessential disconnection resister. He was autistic, which means the inability to connect with some things, while obsessively connecting to others. He was not able to connect socially, but names, including all the ones in the phone book, were his constant companions.

Statistics are also powerful weapons for those of us trapped in the colorless world of "black *or* white." Things are seldom one *or* the other. Here again, the limited world of duality puts a boundary between two polarities; separates the twins; and bifurcates the truth. This is probably why angry people seldom discuss how they feel. Think about it. The last time you were in an argument, did anybody mention how they honestly felt? The discussion was probably limited to "just the facts." The universal disagreement is usually based on statements like, "But you said." If you ever want to confuse an angry person, shift the focus of the subject at hand from facts to feelings then stand back and watch the fun.

Compassion

Two watchdogs at the temple of *anger* are judgment and punishment. Both reinforce the never-ending process of resistance, disconnection, and war. Agreement and compassion, on the other hand, can bring about a truce faster than the most formidable opponent. Having experienced the sheer pleasure of acknowledging that an adversary may have a point, can lead you from anger to peace.

This old Indian legend, supposedly true, is a case in point. Once there was an old man of the Hopi Indian tribe. He was reputed to be 105 years old. A reporter from one of the big city newspapers came to the reservation to interview him.

"What do you eat?" asked the reporter.

"Nothing special—the same as everyone else in the tribe," the old man replied.

"Oh, come now," quipped the newsman. "You've got to eat something different."

"No," stated the native. "I do just what everyone else in the tribe does. I live by the same laws and obey the same rules. I respect all of God's creation and *I argue with no one.*"

"That's a very laudable trait," said the newsman. "However, you must eat or drink something that's responsible for your longevity. How about the sacred mushroom? Do you eat those by yourself, perhaps?"

"No," said the Hopi. "I eat only what my brothers eat."

"What about fire water? Do you ever have any of that?"

"No," replied the Indian, "neither have any of the other men in the tribe. It's against our laws."

"See here!" the frustrated newsman demanded. "There must be something that you ingest or inhale that accounts for your long life."

The old man looked at his inquisitor for a moment, saw no point arguing, smiled, and then said quietly, "You know, you *may* be right."

Relationships

Since *anger* and *compassion* both need an object, it's no wonder they are most at home in relationships. Relationships are the primary playground for the game of *validation/invalidation*. Those of us with an aversion to invalidation or an addiction to our separate identification will have difficulty with relationship. We will invalidate ourselves by accepting the blame for another's feelings, or invalidate and blame another for our feelings. The tendency to put responsibility *on* or take responsibility *for* another can be the single greatest roadblock in the path of a beautiful relationship. One of the most difficult rules to remember in any relationship is *the need to put responsibility on, or take responsibility for another, is in direct proportion to the inability to take responsibility for one's self.* Blaming another for the way we feel is not only inaccurate but an admission of refusing to accept responsibility for ourselves. It also shows a lack of *compassion*. The mother who discovers that her unmarried daughter is pregnant and moans, "How could she do this *to me*?" is a shining example. As absurd as it sounds, it's not all that unusual.

Codependent relationships are another example. They consist of two disconnected people, both demanding the other person give them a feeling they refuse to give themselves. When two people get together with this commitment and cater to one another's addiction/aversion pattern, they end up being codependent and neither one dependable.

Our addiction to being a separate, independent self, therefore needing to *connect*, is the basis of our difficulty in this mode.

Welcome to the world of *connecting*. In this mode *our number one priority is connection. Our first inclination is to place blame. Our main consideration is with our identification.*

✦ ✦ ✦

Reminder: Connecting and disconnecting are of vital importance in this mode. Once we eliminate the mental barrier between the two, we recognize that we must disconnect in order to connect. We perform this ritual of connecting and disconnecting literally billions of times each day. It's only when we attempt to avoid disconnecting that we bring the ritual's natural cycle to a screaming halt. It's our avoidance, not the disconnection that causes our discomfort.

✦ ✦ ✦

Victimized/Fairly Treated

Our society has recently become incredibly adroit at being victims. We just need to look at the lawsuits for spilled coffee, icy sidewalks, and inexplicit labels to get the hint. The most outrageous was a woman who put her dog in the microwave to dry it after its bath. The dog, of course, imploded, and the woman sued the manufacturer for not specifically warning against drying pets in their machine. She was awarded two million dollars. How could this happen? We have all developed such an aversion to feeling victimized, that such travesties are not only allowed but encouraged.

Hal's mother always managed to be victimized. She was a wizard at finding people and situations she could use for playing the victim. If there was a crooked stockbroker, she would hire him. If there was a dishonest lawyer, she would get him or her to take her case. One of the most proficient surgeons in the country made a once-in-a-lifetime mistake while removing her appendix.

Hal was always running home to rescue her from her mishaps. One day while recovering from an illness, she climbed up on a rickety old chair to get a waffle iron from the top of the cupboard. She fell and broke her leg. Hal rushed home again but this time was able to witness her victim pattern quite clearly. He took her to the emergency room and told her she'd have to find a ride home on her own. "Anyone who did what you just did, doesn't deserve to be rescued. I have great compassion for your need to be a victim, but I'm not going to encourage it"—and he didn't. As long as there was no one around to play opposite her "Poor Pitiful Pauline," her number of accidents decreased dramatically.

Right/Wrong

This story illustrates how letting go of what we believe is right, is sometimes the most correct thing we can do.

One day a minister was walking along the beach of a lovely South Sea island when he saw a few natives weaving with palm fronds. Approaching them, he struck up a conversation. The natives were delighted to meet the minister, and three of them informed him that they too, were Christians. They had taken instruction from a man of the cloth several years before. The minister was pleased and asked them if they knew the Lord's Prayer. "What's that?" they replied. The minister was shocked. He promptly informed them they couldn't honestly call themselves Christians unless they knew the Lord's Prayer.

"What do you say when you pray?" the minister inquired.

"Oh, we bow our heads and say, 'We are three. You are three. Bless us.'"

The minister was aghast at the heretical training. He vowed to teach the poor misguided souls and bring them into the fold. He spent all that day and the next going over the Lord's Prayer. While they were not terribly quick, the natives were so willing it was not difficult for the minister. The following evening, to repay his effort, the natives came down to the boat to see him off and dutifully recited the Lord's Prayer for him. They did it without a single mistake and the minister was very proud.

Years later, the very same minister happened to pass the very same island. He stood on the deck of the boat, remembering his religious charges, pleased that he had, in a way, helped them with their Christian education. All at once he heard the deckhands in a tumultuous uproar. As he walked around to uncover the trouble, he saw a great beam of light to one side of the ship. At closer inspection, he observed his old native friends, walking on top of the water approaching the ship. The minister leaned over the side in utter disbelief. Just then his three friends recognized him and said, "Oh, kind minister, we are so glad to have found you. We have waited so long for you. We have forgotten the beautiful prayer you so kindly taught us. We remember only a few lines and are so disappointed that we are not able to be of credit to your fine teaching. Please help us again to remember those sacred words."

After the minister recovered his senses and was able to speak, he looked at the shining faces and glowing eyes of the natives and said, "My dear friends go home. When you wish to talk to God, just bow your heads and repeat, 'We are three. You are three. Bless us.'"

Acknowledged/Unacknowledged

Helen had a tremendous aversion to being overlooked. She disliked it so much that no explanation could convince her of its merits. All the discussion about not being noticed if you wanted to remain anonymous or not being called on to deliver some information you didn't have made not the slightest impression. Then, one day, she was waiting in line for a bus with six other people when a drunken "street person" came staggering up to the seven of them. He was verbally abusive and brandished a small pocket knife. He proceeded to go down the line insulting each of the people waiting there—until he came to Helen. For some unknown reason, it was as though she were invisible. He addressed the three people to her right and the three to her left, and overlooked her completely. From that moment on, she never doubted the validity and value of being overlooked.

Any time we resist a feeling, but sincerely want to see its merits, we will find some scenario to help us. As absurd as it might be, there is an answer to every question. We just have to be open enough and in the moment, to hear it when it arrives.

Separation

There is no way we will ever eliminate anger from our lives, nor should we. It's our warning signal that we're blaming someone or something for our own responsibility—our feelings. We don't like them, to be sure, and it's much easier to place the responsibility on someone else. It's not, however, a gesture of awareness or happiness, and if that's what we truly want, blame is not the road to take. Neither is the identification with a separate, individual persona. Once we have been able to connect with all of ourselves, accept all that we are and all that we might be, we can begin to unite with others. We'll notice our path is coupled and joined, linked and bridged with every other path on the planet.

Separation is and always was a child of our imagination. Each time we trick ourselves into believing someone or something is not a part of us, we have attached to some individual thing, and detached from the rest of the world, or at least tried to. "Try" is all we can ever do, because we can only pretend we aren't a part of everything there is, whether we like it or not.

✦ ✦ ✦

We are in danger
as long as we are at peace
in our separateness.

No Bad Feelings!
PARTIII

✦ ✦ ✦

CHAPTER 12

Where Do We Go From Here?

The obvious answer is another question. *Where do we want to go?* In a survey of our seminar participants, more than five thousand people were asked that question and less than 18 percent were able to answer it. When quizzed as to what they wanted more than anything else in life, the overwhelming response was, "I don't know." Many people said, "happiness," but when asked what would make them happy, "I don't know," was the hands-down favorite. It's interesting to realize that none of us will go to the market, the drugstore, or the gas station without knowing what we want to buy when we get there. Yet, many of us will go on about our lives without the slightest idea what it is we want from life—or what we're willing to pay.

Conversely, the majority of us can answer instantly what it is that we want to *avoid* in our lives. Imagine planning a vacation with only the input of where you don't want to go, and what you don't want to see. Still, many of us plan our lives in exactly that fashion. Consequently, the first thing we need to know, if we're looking for happiness, is exactly what it is to which we attach our happiness, and to what we are really committed.

Wanting and being committed are not the same thing. We may want a million dollars, but until we go out and devote all our time and energy earning it, we're not committed. There's an old expression, "The difference between involvement and commitment is like the difference between ham and eggs. With eggs, the hen is only involved. With ham, the pig is truly committed."

Commitments

Our commitments are the cornerstones of our lives, and everything, yes everything mirrors and supports those commitments. While claiming we're committed to one thing, we are often really committed to something else.

Let's go back to the traffic jam again. When we find ourselves trapped in gridlock, it's usually at the very time we're in a hurry to get somewhere. We tell ourselves we're committed to arriving at our destination on time, when we're actually committed to avoiding being late. We're not facing an addiction to punctuality but an aversion to tardiness that led us to great frustration while in the traffic jam. How do we know? Otherwise, we would not have been so frustrated while having been there. Remember—we always get the feeling that we want or the feeling we want to avoid, whichever want is the stronger.

We Can't Commit to a Noun

One important thing to keep in mind is that we cannot commit to a noun, a person, a thing, and so forth—only to a verb.

✦ ✦ ✦

Reminder: This may sound outrageous, because it is so common to say "I'm committed to my job, my relationship, my sport, and so forth." We're not saying this is wrong, just incomplete. Delve into the feelings behind the job, relationship, and sport to open new options for clarity and joy.

✦ ✦ ✦

We often think we're committed to a situation, but what we're really committed to is the feeling behind it. For example, we cannot commit to a relationship—only to protecting, destroying, questioning, continuing, undermining, enjoying, changing, and so forth, the relationship. A commitment is never to a goal but how we approach a goal. When we say we're committed to a job or a spouse, we haven't begun to uncover our real commitment. To do so, we need to ask ourselves, "To what am I committed in the job environment? Am I committed to being productive in my job?" We need to ask ourselves what we are experiencing at the moment, then, witness what we are feeling, and witness what we are avoiding feeling. That will clarify the very thing and the only thing to which we are committed. Once we are aware of our real commitment, we're free to pursue it or change it.

Jack was a superior gymnastic coach. The high school was proud of him and his students adored him. He had planned the spring meet with great care, claiming his true commitment was to the safety of all the participants. Many of the other coaches offered to help him, but he would accept none. He was going to be in control, even if he had to do everything himself, which, in fact, he did. He worked from 10 A.M. to 10 P.M. and totally exhausted himself. After the meet was over, it was discovered that one of the uneven bars had not been checked and was about to come loose. Had it done so, a gymnast could have been severely injured. Jack suddenly realized that he was not committed to safety or even feeling in control. He was committed to fighting feeling out of control, and it almost brought about the very thing he most wanted to avoid.

We Are Constantly Recommitting

Commitment requires constant reaffirmation. No commitment is etched in stone. We commit and recommit a thousand times each day. Everything we do, every word we utter, every thought that passes through our consciousness is an affirmation of some commitment. Many times we're not aware of it, but it's there nonetheless. When we commit to finding fault, everything we see has to do with fault. Abraham Maslow said, "When the only tool you have is a hammer, everything looks like a nail." When we commit to enjoying, everything in our line of vision becomes a cause for celebration. When we commit to understanding, the most involved process becomes crystal clear. When we commit to fighting misunderstanding, the simplest explanation assumes monumental complications.

When we look in the mirror in the morning and think, "If that SOB says that to me one more time, I'll…"—that is a commitment to fighting whatever feeling we experience when that SOB says whatever he says. When we look at a sunset and smile, chances are that we are committed to enjoying the feeling we use the sunset to symbolize.

One interesting sideline is that when we're committed to fighting, we can only remember things with resistance. When we're committed to accepting, we are only able to remember things with approval. When we're expanding, we think only in terms of expansion. When contracting, we can't recall expansion at all. Even though we've experienced both, we're only able to experience what we're committed to at the moment. Everything happens for the best, only when we're committed to experiencing the best. Things happen for the worst when we're committed to fighting the worst.

Everything Supports Our Commitment

One of the greatest side benefits of being aware of our commitments is recognizing that there are no wrong decisions.

◆ ◆ ◆

Reminder: As ridiculous a statement as that may first appear, consider that whatever choice we make, it is made to support whatever we are committed to at that given moment. That's why the decision is always the correct one. It's the right one for that particular commitment. When we see it as an incorrect decision it is because later we're looking at it with a different commitment.

✦ ✦ ✦

If we keep leading ourselves to relationships with people who are unsupportive, and it bothers us, we can be fairly certain that our commitment has not been to feeling supported. The benevolent universe, has complied with our commitment and given us situations where we can continue to fight feeling unsupported, since that's our real commitment.

Committing to being happy, being aware, and being joyful all take arduous discipline. We may start out making happiness our number one priority, but the minute the threat of feeling invalidated, left out, inadequate, or purposeless appears, our priority goes out the window. The frustrating part of the process is that most of the time we don't even see what we're doing. Consequently, the first exercise, or bit of practice, is to take a good hard look at our commitments, our priorities. If we don't know what we want, what we don't want will have all our attention.

Process 1: Clarifying Priorities
A

This process is divided into three parts. All three are similar, but all are essential. Write down five things you want most in your life. If you can't think of five, write as many as you can. Prioritize the list by marking 1 next to the one you want the most, then continue through 5, the one you want least. Then start at the bottom of the list and say, "In order to have 4 (whatever 4 is), I'd be willing to give up 5 (whatever 5 is) forever." Be sure to say "forever," and be sure to make the declaration out loud. There's some commitment that happens when the statement is vocal. If you find the statement is not true, reverse it. "In order to have 5, I'd be willing to give up 4 forever." Then

4 becomes 5. If neither seems true, pick one. You have to make a choice, or the process won't work. Pretend that a spaceship is leaving for one of two planets—you can go to 5 or 4, but not both. Then reprioritize your list if necessary. Keep going up the list. "In order to have 3, I'd be willing to give up 4 forever." Continue until you have a 1.

Here is a hint for possible difficulties along the way: If one of the 5 priorities is something akin to, "I want my wife to stop nagging me," the process won't work. Part A is about what you want, not what you want to avoid.

Why go through this whole process? Why not just write the list and prioritize it? Because, for some unknown reason, hearing yourself vocalize, and use the word "forever" makes it an experience rather than a concept. You may be surprised at how often the priorities rearrange themselves. This is process 1-A.

B

Make a list of five things you would like to avoid, or erase from your life. Write 1 next to the biggest aversion and 5 next to the least bothersome. Then continue as you did in 1-A. Only this time, the wording changes slightly: "In order to avoid 4, I'd be willing to accept 5 forever." This is where the "forever" will really make a difference. Continue using this phrase as you go up this list.

If, in part B, you have a priority that states "I want God to rid the world of cancer," it won't work either. Not because we spoke to God and He refused, but because you need to discover the feeling behind the situation you're trying to avoid. It could be feeling powerless to help those in need. It could be a wish to eliminate something you believe is wrong. It could simply be your aversion to feeling victimized. This is process 1-B.

C

Now comes the real test. Here's where you see where your true commitment lies. You'll need to compare lists. First, identify the feeling that goes with 1 on your A list, and the feeling that goes with 1 on your B list. Then say, "In order to have 1 on the A list and the feeling that goes with it, I'll be willing to accept 1 on the B list and the feeling that goes with it forever." If that works for you, you can be certain you are running to the angels. If 1 on the B list takes priority, you will at least be able to identify the goblins you're running from.

Keep these lists available and see how closely you honor them each day. You may use this process for any list you wish to prioritize or decision you want to make. "In order to get this job, I'm willing to give up certain conveniences *forever.*" It's main purpose here, however, is to help you begin to see what your real commitments in life are, and just what you've made more important than what you say will make you happy.

Our Most Precious Moment

Since fear always lives in the future and pain's home is in the past, it would appear that the most logical place to reside, if we're looking for happiness and peace of mind, is in the present. All expectations and goals and possible failures lie ahead of us. All unpleasant things said and done are behind us. We're *all* aware of that. Why then, do we seldom remain in the moment? Quite frankly, no one has ever come up with a completely definitive answer. Oh, it's obvious we've been told to "think ahead, plan ahead, and remember the past," but why did we follow those suggestions when we've ignored so many others? One of the most credible guesses is that being out of the moment has become a habit. Why? So we can avoid whatever feeling we're experiencing here and now.

Case in point: If someone says something invalidating to us, rather than experiencing a feeling we don't like we come up with a scenario about why the invalidating person shouldn't have said what he or she did. That way, we can concentrate on what *was*, rather than how we are feeling at this very moment. The same process applies to expectations and goals. We'd much rather think about how wonderful something is *going* to be, than deal with the difficulties getting there.

Think for a minute about how we respond when our expectation isn't met. We may wallow in disappointment about something that has occurred hours ago. We trap ourselves in time with expressions like, "As soon as I get my check, then I'll feel safe," or "As soon as this job is finished, then I'll feel satisfied." We forget that the "comfortable" feeling has a better chance of being around in the next moment if we're willing to practice it now.

One of the cardinal truths connected to living in the moment is—both happiness and unhappiness are habits. Consequently, the more we practice one or the other, the more it will take center stage. Chances are, what we are doing *this* moment is what we've made a habit of doing all our lives.

One habit most of us have acquired is one of always being in a hurry. There never seems to be enough time. Many of the things we say are our priorities get postponed until after *this* gets done or *that* is finished. Postponement is one of the most popular reasons for not being in the moment. People in a hurry are never in the moment, and the moment is the only place where they can feel. Consequently, people who are in a hurry are not aware of what they're feeling, at least not at that moment. This is a good thing to keep in mind when we're trying to communicate feelings to someone on the run.

Lest you think that living in just this moment might be limiting, remember that *everything exists in the moment when only the moment exists.* It's the "when only the moment exists," that's important. So many of us keep living the same moment over and over. It's as though we haven't lived, let's say fifty years, but have lived the thirtieth year over twenty times. The only real entertainment is going on right now, this very minute, and the dullest thing we could do is keep playing reruns. How do we learn to switch from "then" to "now"? By applying process 2 as often as possible.

Process 2: At This Moment

It's a short one, but for the best results should be done many times a day. If you can do it at least three times a day, within three weeks you'll make a difference in the way you perceive yourself and your surroundings.

Stop whatever you're doing and sit quietly for ten seconds. Then ask yourself the following three questions:

1. What am I doing now, both externally and internally?
2. Is there anything I really *want* at this moment?
3. Is there anything I really want to *avoid* at this moment?

Here are two examples our friend Pam shared from her experience. She was saying that when she "plays" the answers are quite different than when she "works."

While downhill skiing:

1. What am I doing?
   Externally: "I'm riding the mountain."
   Internally: "I'm celebrating freedom."
2. Is there anything I really *want* at this moment?
   "I just want to keep celebrating."
3. Is there anything I want to *avoid?*
   "I'm not remotely aware of any avoidance."

While driving to a client's office to make a presentation:

1. What am I doing?
   Externally: "I'm driving the car."
   Internally: "I'm mentally rehearsing my sales pitch."
2. Is there anything I really *want* at this moment?
   "I want to look good, perform well, and get the sale!"
3. Is there anything I want to *avoid?*
   "I want to avoid looking stupid and losing the sale!"

Pam discovered that when she "worked," she needed to control the outcome. She was deeply concerned with an end result. We pointed out that an aversion is usually behind need-ing to control the situation. She asked, "How can you tell the difference between going toward what you want, and avoid-ing what you don't want?" We suggested she review the material on addictions and aversions in Chapter 6. Also, the easiest answer is based on whether you are fully in the mo-ment or not. While Pam is skiing she is in the moment and going toward what she wants. When she is doing business she is often out of the moment and into controlling the outcome. That is when she is running from what she doesn't want to happen. This simple "in or out of the moment" question can be used by all of us. Some people will find they are more "in the moment" while at work, and more controlling while play-ing sports. A golf tournament is a good example.

We reminded Pam that everything exists in the moment when only the moment exists. She decided she would like to approach more of her "work" the same way she approached "play." That would allow her to listen better, respond more clearly, and find the thrill of the process. She had experienced a few real highs of being in the moment with business, but they were relatively few for all the years she had been work-ing. We assured her no one lives 100 percent of the time in the moment; but to be able to go in and out more gracefully would be quite a reward.

Another way of deciding if you're going toward or run-ning from, is the intensity of your urge. The stronger the drive, the stronger the chance of aversion. The man who *has to* inter-rupt every ten minutes to show how much he knows, is really fighting anyone guessing how little he knows. The woman who *demands* a show of respect is usually covering up a fight with disrespect. Whenever there is "protesting too much" there is aversion.

Ask yourself the three questions. Can you find those mo-ments where you *want* nothing and want to *avoid* nothing? Those are the moments when the angels are close by. When you are caught up in the *wanting* and *avoiding*, at least you'll see what it is you're making your number 1 commitment. Remember—what you resist persists.

Once you are aware of what your commitment truly is, you can make an informed decision about where you want to go next. What angels do you want to run to, or what goblins are you trying to outrun?

Process 3: Observational Meditation

This type of meditation may be quite different from the practices you have encountered before. It can take place while you're sitting on a bus, taking a walk, or looking in the face of a loved one. You don't have to assume any specific position, although the more comfortable you can make yourself, the easier and more successful the process will be. You don't have to learn anything, imagine anything, or say anything. All you have to do is be quiet and watch what's happening. Listen to how your "drunken monkey" mind is chattering. *Just listen!* You don't have to do anything about what you're hearing. You certainly don't have to try to silence your mind. If you do, you'll fall asleep, and that's not the objective. Simply be aware of what's going on in your head. Observe. Don't become involved with the thoughts. They're just thoughts, after all. If you can be the "watcher," "the observer," and "the audience," you'll soon be able to shift from the present moment into the eternal moment. There is a difference.

The best and quickest way to explain it is that the present moment is contained in our thoughts, while the eternal moment is in between our thoughts. That's where the real joy is. That's where our ultimate peace of mind resides—in between our thoughts. We can't force ourselves to go there, we can't force ourselves to think, or not think anything. However, when we allow ourselves to simply follow what is happening, moment by moment, the travel accommodations take care of themselves.

The fascinating part of this practice is that after a length of time, things begin to happen. Things change. We become more accepting. Our feelings are clearer and less contrary, because we've become more flexible. How does simply watching something change it? Werner Heisenberg, as far back as 1927, said, "The observer alters the observed by the mere act of observation." His cohort, John A. Wheeler, stated, "We must replace the term 'observer' with the term 'participator.'" Physicist Stephen Wolensky claims, "Things come into existence only when we observe them." So it would seem that observational meditation can be responsible for quite a lot of happenings.

Meditation is one of the greatest arts in life. Maybe it's *the* greatest, and nobody can possibly teach it to us. When we learn to truly see ourselves, to observe our feelings and how we fight them or celebrate them, that's meditation. Meditation is not concentration, which is exclusion and requires resistance. Meditation is hard work. It demands the highest form of discipline. But it's a pretty straight path to loving, and loving is the best guarantee of happiness we could want.

Process 4: Going Beyond Resistance

Possibly the greatest frustration in dealing with resistance is letting it go. The sixty-four-thousand-dollar question inevitably arises in the form of "Okay, so I know I'm resisting feeling misunderstood. How do I stop resisting?" The answer is, "You don't stop. You go beyond it." "Isn't that the same thing? Isn't it just a question of semantics?" Indeed not. *Going through and out the other side of an experience is vastly different from trying to get rid of it.*

The technique of going beyond resistance is relatively simple, but you have to want to do it. You have to make it more important than your need to resist. If this is the case, the first step is to determine just what feeling you're resisting. This is the same process as the one you might use in letting go of a stiffness in a muscle. Once you've recognized where the resistance is, let's say in your shoulders, you pull your shoulders up toward your ears and tighten the muscles as much as you can. You tighten, tighten, tighten, and then let go. Magically, the stiffness subsides. The process is exactly the same for an emotional stiffness. Once you've zeroed in on the feeling, you start the resistance in earnest—with all your might. "Damn, nobody understands me. I hate feeling misunderstood. I wish there were no such thing on the face of the earth as understanding and misunderstanding. I hate feeling misunderstood more than I love life." Really get into it. And stay focused on your resistance to the feeling rather than going off about the characters in a situation that mirrored your resistance. This is *your fight with the feeling.*

Three minutes of this serious workout should do it. Once you have reached the extreme of your resistance, then you are able to let it go. It's as though something in the universe takes over and you magically pop out the other side. It's much like diving into a vortex in a stream. Once you reach the centrifugal force, you are catapulted out the other side. Whether it's a stream, shoulder stiffness, or a feeling you'd do most anything to avoid, *you have to go through it to get beyond it.*

How you go through your resistance will reflect your own individual style. One way is to express it outwardly. In verbalizing and acting out our resistance we let the energy of the fight carry us to greater clarity. This works if we prefer having a sounding board to bring everything into consciousness.

Another style is to work it through internally. This approach is for those who are distracted by their own outward expression and find clarity by going within.

Explosions are sometimes quick and powerful, while "mulling" and "sleeping on it" may be slower and quieter. However, the end result and the extent of the transition are equal.

You will find your own combination of inward and outward processing that best serves you. Some of you may wish to write it all out in a journal. Going through the resistance rather than trying to get rid of it is the key issue.

The most difficult part of this whole process is taking re-sponsibility for your resistance. We often hear remarks like, "A wave of resistance just came over me." No matter how hard you protest, no one has waved a magic wand and brought on your resistance. *You* put it there, and *you're* the only one who can let it go. No one can take it away or even prescribe relief. You are 100 percent responsible for doing what you're doing— and changing what you're doing.

Living joyously and being happy is an enormous commit-ment. It's a lot of hard work. Once we've dived into the pool of resistance, we have to swim to the other side or we'll drown in our own battle. One comforting revelation though, is that ev-eryone in the world has to go through this same process. Nobody gets out of the water without some pretty heavy strok-ing. Whether it's back paddle or sidestroke, we all have to commit heavily if we want to get to the other side. There are, of course, those who just want to keep busy resisting, avoid-ing, and denying. They're the prime example of the old cigarette commercial, "I'd rather fight than switch." Good for them. They've made their choice. Nothing wrong with it. We've all known people whose only joy in life seems to be to confront, contradict, and complain. We see them in the pool all the time don't we?

✦ ✦ ✦

*The most important
part of any one practice
is the practicing.*

CHAPTER 13

✦ ✦ ✦

What's Love Got to Do
With All This?

Suppose we *do* unify the feeling pairs? Suppose we *do* integrate all our emotions, and *are* able to experience everything as part of our process, and not want to change it? Then what? Then we are able to experience something that can't be put into words. It's the exact opposite of the story of the little boy who was drawing a picture and when his mother asked what he was drawing, he simply replied, "God." His amused parent explained to him that he couldn't really do that since no one knew what God looked like. Without any concern, or missing a beat, the youngster assured her, "They will, after I finish this picture."

We can't begin to put on paper or vocalize this experience. It simply has no name, and while it can't really be compared to any other experience, it comes closest to *love*. However, unlike what most of us consider love, it has no object. You might say that it is loving, but loving nothing in particular, loving everything. Perhaps it is unconditional, the love that passes all understanding. Ecstasy might do it. Samadhi, Kensho,

153

Epiphany are all candidates. However, like any experience, naming or defining it takes something away.

Most of us are eons away from unconditional loving. We place one of the four following conditions on our love and happiness. In raw, unvarnished terms, we say:

1. I won't be happy or loving if things are not up to my standards.

Or

2. I won't be happy or loving if things don't meet my expectations.

Or

3. I won't be happy or loving if I can't achieve my end result.

Or

4. I won't be happy or loving if people won't agree with what I see.

Or all of the above.

Funny thing about love: we forget that we can love things without wanting to own them. We can love people without wanting to manipulate them; and we can love ourselves without wanting to change a thing. In fact, any other kind of love really isn't love.

Why don't more of us love this way more of the time? Perhaps it's because, as children, when most of us reached a feeling that we resisted, instead of being taught how to recognize and make friends with it, we were told to fight it. Or at best, ignore it, or deny it and it would go away. When a balloon popped, we were distracted from our feeling of loss. When we were embarrassed, we were quickly reassured so we could avoid feeling not good enough. To help this completely ineffectual process, we were given a toy as a distraction or even a reward for trying to get rid of a feeling. After a while, it's no wonder we came to believe that a toy, a candy, or some other object would bring us comfort. It never did.

Overeaters Anonymous members will confirm that this kind of comfort seldom lasts long. Maybe that's why we're still looking for that magic symbol. A teenager's craving for the latest music video—an executive's obsession with the most recent gimmick—are all examples of how, when we aren't loving, we look for something else to fill the void.

Rather than a sonic boom, love is more like a soft breeze wiping away all the cobwebs and illusions. It makes a kind of sense, that when we let go of all of our attachments/aversions/identifications, we have let go of all that's material. With that accomplished, there's nothing left—nothing you can see, hear, or name. All that's left is Spirit and consciousness. That is in a way, what you feel, because that's who you are.

✦ ✦ ✦

Do not search for love.
Just let go of everything
that is in the way.

CHAPTER 14

✦ ✦ ✦

A Fable…An Angel Story With a Moral

Christine is seventy-five years old and still believes in angels. She always has. Her mother used to write notes from the angels, and quietly slip them by her bed each night. Christine knew that the penmanship did not belong to some celestial being but was that of her own dear mother. It didn't make any difference. She always did whatever the angels asked. (Her mother had a real thing going for her.) She never thought of angels as tiny creatures with wings and halos, even though that's an appealing symbol. Her angels were not nearly so whimsical or unpredictable. They were the monitors responsible for her "feel good" perceptions of life.

They have since been given names—not individual but categorical. Psychologists glimpse them as "mood swings." Drug users have met them in "highs." Endocrinologists refer to them as "endorphin-related experiences." There are no specific chemical formulas for them, but according to most biological monitoring devices, they *do* exist. They are, in short, the symbols for syncronystic happenings and our otherwise sudden and unexplainable happiness. If we go along with the endo-

157

crinological title, there would have to be the coffee angel, the chocolate angel, and the sex angel—all of whom add to our feeling of well-being.

The one dubious piece of this rational explanation of an irrational puzzle is the feeling of ecstasy that arrives when there is no discernable substance or activity to invite it. A questionable clue may be that often it's not the presence of something but the *absence* of something that zaps our pleasure button. That, believe it or not, might just be the work of the angels.

They could be showing us that when we let go of something we've been clutching for a long time, we feel better. When we're willing to part with an attachment, we feel lighter and freer. Isn't it possible that every time we let go of an attachment, addiction, or aversion, the delicious feeling we experience may be ushered in by what could be called "an angel"? It could be called anything. It often is.

The entire meaning in this seemingly "far out" diatribe is that we can call anything by any name, and it will not expand or diminish it one little bit. The desire to let go and get out of our own way may be the result of a deep seated psycho-physical experience, or the work of the angels. Both may be conjecture but neither can be proven. Nothing to do with feelings can be proven because they are not objects, not totally definable, and therefore unprovable. They are part of our process of living—an enormous part.

Whenever we are able to accept a heretofore avoided feeling, and we have a pleasant sensation, we might say that our body chemistry has shifted, our right brain hemisphere has a higher alpha-theta production, or that an angel has brought a change. Does it really matter? Are we stuck on a particular identification? If we experience the bliss of oneness, unity consciousness, emptiness, or transcendence, do we really care what it is called? If we don't believe in angels, all well and good. Then why are we running from goblins?

Once we realize that letting go of boundaries, duality, and separation leads to joy, and it can happen at any time, anywhere, we're not concerned with the nomenclature. We all know the joy and celebration of a party, the inspiration of a moment without judgment. We know too the joy and celebration of the silence when standing by a snow-capped mountain with the absence of distractions. The ability to do both is a blessing. However, to also find the beauty, perfection, and excitement in a ghetto or an understaffed old folk's home is to step inside, even for a moment, divine consciousness and true spirit, home of the endorphins and the angels. The need to change nothing and enjoy what is, is not only blissful, but a contagious awareness as well. It is infectious, and unchecked, can metastasize to every corner of the earth. We can initiate this process, and the angels will help whether we believe in them or not.

✦ ✦ ✦

*We can never be
disappointed conversing
at length with angels.*

CHAPTER 15

The Rest Is Up To You

Since most authors like the last word, and we wouldn't dream of leaving you stranded, here are a dozen hints to follow when you need a little reminder.

Whenever you're in a difficult situation, look for the feeling behind it. Ask yourself, "If the worst possible thing happened, how would I feel, and just what feeling would I be resisting?" How do you know that you're resisting? Simply by the fact that the situation is a difficult one. Acceptance never breeds difficulty.

1. Whenever you feel the need to do something, check and see if you're moving toward or running from something. If you are driven, if it is something you *must* do, chances are you're resisting how you'd feel if you didn't do it. If you see someone forcing his intelligence, he's probably avoiding his incompetence.

2. Whenever you feel stressed, look and see what it is you want to control, change, manipulate, improve, and so forth. These are all signs of resistance. Remember that it's the *resistance* to the situation and the feeling behind it, not the situation or the feeling, that's causing the stress.

3. Whenever you are feeling less than loving, peaceful, or compassionate, ask yourself, "What have I made more important than feeling loving, peaceful, or compassionate?" This is how you've chosen to feel.

4. Whenever you are upset with an object or a person, remember that they are merely a *symbol* of the feeling you're upset about. Why take it out on them?

5. Whenever you're feeling high, remember that it's going to be followed by a low. Even more important, when you're in a low, remember it's going to be followed by a high.

6. Whenever you find yourself wanting approval from someone, remind yourself that it's the approval that you're not giving yourself. The same goes for validation, security, respect, and so forth. Whenever you're aware of fighting a feeling, remind yourself, "I'd rather fight feeling (fill in the blank) than be happy."

7. Notice how often you complain, criticize, contradict, or compare. They are all preludes to some form of discomfort.

8. Every now and then, see how it feels to listen with no judgment, no opinion, no preference, and no expectation. You'll be astonished at what you'll hear.

9. At least once each day, spend ten minutes being aware of what you're thinking. Watch your thoughts, then let them go. Remember, they do not define you. They're just thoughts.

10. Keep in mind that any difficulty, pain, discomfort, or confusion is the direct result of resistance, avoidance, or aversion.

Good luck!

✦ ✦ ✦

There is a place, as far beyond love,
as love is beyond hate.
It is this place from whence we came.
It is to this place where we are destined to return.
From time to time within our lives
We are privileged to glimpse these fair Elysian fields,
these golden valleys,
Nestled in the protective shadows
of paternal mountains
with maternal love.
These moments we call "bliss."

KEY THOUGHTS TO REMEMBER

✦ ✦ ✦

- All human behavior is built on feelings.
- Feelings come in pairs and you can't have one without the other.
- Our life does not depend upon what happens, but upon how we feel about what happens.
- We cannot feel another's feelings any more than they can feel ours.
- The instant we've created one feeling, we've created its twin.
- In order to experience one feeling, we must be willing to experience the other.
- What we resist almost always persists and yet we keep resisting.
- There are no bad feelings.
- The symptoms of fighting are pain, fatigue, and confusion.
- The symptoms of accepting are clarity, abundance, and freedom.
- Coping is a form of resignation that is really passive resistance.
- Situations may expedite or exacerbate feelings, but they don't create them. They are only symbols of our feelings.

- When an inner situation is not made conscious, it happens outside as coincidence.
- Feelings are the matrix of all thought.
- You always get the feeling you want or the feeling you want to avoid, whichever is the stronger.
- Addictions are things we can't live without.
- Aversions are things we can't live with.
- We are attached to our aversions.
- An addiction is a temporary relief from an aversion.
- Trust is allowing things to happen rather than trying to make them happen.
- The big trick in the Having mode is practicing how to really have.
- Nobody likes or dislikes us. They only like or dislike the person they've created to fit their own scenario.
- The need to put responsibility on, or take responsibility for another, is in direct proportion to the inability to take responsibility for oneself.
- Both happiness and unhappiness are habits.
- Everything exists in the moment when only the moment exists.
- All human behavior is built on feelings.

ABOUT THE AUTHORS

✦ ✦ ✦

June Spencer is a true renaissance woman. Her careers have spanned art and medicine, research and entertainment. She has been rated as one of the top ten women in three different fields of endeavor.

As a young woman, June was a copywriter, a fashion commentator, and a model, appearing in *Vogue* and *Harpers Bazaar*. During World War II, she worked as a psychiatric nurse. While raising two children, she found time to appear in over 2,000 television commercials, and played leading roles in two daytime serials, *The Secret Storm* and *The Guiding Light*, plus several Off-Broadway productions.

In 1971 she began a career in parapsychology and became an instructor in the pioneer self-development course, the Silva Method. There she met and married Jim Spencer, who is 24 years her junior. Together they have authored four books. Years of studying all the major world religions has led to their ordination as Inter-Faith Ministers at the Communion of Souls Seminary.

June is not only a gifted writer, but a challenging teacher and charismatic lecturer as well.

✦ ✦ ✦

Jim Spencer's academic work is in the field of psychology—with particular focus on family guidance and business psychology. His work experience is diverse: from instructing ice skating at Michigan State University, to sales and marketing for an executive office furniture manufacturer, where he dealt with corporate heads and major architectural firms in New York City. While directing the textile division of the company, Jim became a talented weaver and has produced various commissioned works in New York City.

In 1972, Jim began his studies in parapsychology. He and June started team-teaching the Silva Method in 1976. Their system of instruction was so successful they broadened their work by founding the Let Go & Live Institute in 1977. Using the insights gained through twenty-five years of leading seminars, he and June have spent over 15,000 hours working with more than 8,000 people, helping them to find a happier and more fulfilling lifestyle. They have given lectures and seminars throughout the USA—from the Archdiocese of New Jersey to the Orange County Medical Center in Florida, from the Vietnam Veterans Council to the United Nations. They are an attractive, dynamic couple who obviously practice the excitement and joy of life they preach.

Currently June and Jim celebrate life in the shadow of four 14,000 foot mountain peaks in Nathrop, Colorado.

ACKNOWLEDGMENTS

✦ ✦ ✦

Now that you have finished the book, you can see how thousands of people have influenced the discoveries we have shared with you. *We would like to thank everyone who has ever crossed our path.* Each one has raised questions, given a reassuring smile, presented a pattern of relating that caused us to explore further, or shared insights which stimulated our passion for discovery.

In Oscar-acceptance-speech–style we want to thank some specific people. "We love you. We really love you!" We are only sorry that you will probably never meet them or be enriched by their friendship as we have been.

Elizabeth Grandinetti, corporate human resource manager, lives in Manhattan and applies Let Go & Live in her work. Her support, drive, and determination have carried this book to fruition. Her willingness to examine her feelings and then celebrate life in style is admirable.

Sherrie Villano, interfaith minister and Let Go & Live counselor in Greenwich Village, New York City, has provided much-needed laughter at the absurdities we all create. Her insights, talents, enthusiasm, and no-nonsense questions have contributed beyond words.

We wouldn't be flourishing without the emotional and financial support of Sandra Segal, Ilse Sonnenberg, and Connie Attanasio. Bless you all for allowing us to pursue our dream.

Our love and gratitude to Kaika Clubwala who said this book must be written; Jennifer Bassie who filled our very first seminar; and, Al Tafoya and Pam Nadolsky for wading through early drafts.

Our gratitude also extends to the editors, literary agents, and publishers whose rejection slips gave us ideas of where we needed to expand and simplify our explanations so that even the disinterested reader could relate to the material.

Our admiration goes to the entire staff of About Books, Inc., and Sue Collier for their professional insights and their personal warmth and courtesy. We only wish we had had your expertise from the beginning.

Thanks to the thousands of individuals who brought themselves to our Let Go & Live seminars. We benefited from each one of you. Big hugs to the group that came every week for meditation, discussion, and idea sharing. We are blessed.

Hundreds more aren't mentioned by name but you have a place in our hearts always. And to the person reading this looking for your name because you have added so much, please forgive us for overlooking the obvious. You are appreciated!

Warm wishes,

June and Jim

SUGGESTED READING

✦ ✦ ✦

These have stimulated our growth and discoveries, and we believe they can enhance your life as well.

Aitken, Robert. *The Gateless Barrier.* New York: North Point Press, 1991.

Beck, Charlotte Joko. *Nothing Special.* New York: HarperCollins, 1990.

Boorstein, Sylvia. *It's Easier Than You Think.* San Francisco: Harper San Francisco, 1997.

Capra, Fritjof. *The Tao of Physics,* 3rd Edition. Berkley, California: Shambhala, 1991.

Chodron, Pema. *The Wisdom of No Escape.* Boston: Shambhala, 1991.

Chopra, Deepak. *Ageless Body, Timeless Mind.* New York: Crown Publishing, 1994.

Cleary, Thomas. *The Secret of the Golden Flower.* San Francisco: Harper San Francisco, 1993.

H.H. Dalai Lama. *Path to Bliss.* Somerville, Massachusetts: Wisdom, 1997.

Epstein, Mark. *Thoughts Without a Thinker.* New York: HarperCollins, 1996.

Goldstein, Joseph. *Insight Meditation.* Boston: Shambhala, 1993.

Grof, Stanislav. *Beyond the Brain.* Albany, New York: State University of New York Press, 1985.

Hahn, Thich Nhat. *The Miracle Of Mindfulness.* Boston: Beacon Press, 1975.

Harrison, Steven. *Do Nothing*. New York: Tarcher Putnam, 1997.

Kornfield, Jack. *A Still Forest Pool*. Wheaton, Illinois: Theosophical Publishing House, 1985.

Krishnamurti. *Total Freedom*. New York: HarperCollins, 1996.

Mitchell, Stephen. *Tao Te Ching*. New York: Harper Trade, 1994.

Moore, Thomas. *Care of the Soul*. New York: Harper Trade, 1994.

Quinn, Daniel. *Ishmael*. New York: Bantam Books, 1998.

Rajneesh (Osho). *Above All, Don't Wobble*. 1993.

Singh, Kathleen Dowling. *The Grace in Dying*. San Francisco: Harper San Francisco, 1998.

Smith, Jean. *Everyday Mind*. Berkley, California: Berkley Publishing, 1999.

Talbot, Michael. *The Holographic Universe*. New York: Harper Trade, 1992.

Tolle, Eckhart. *The Power of Now*. Novato, California: New World Library, 1999.

Walsh, Neal Douglas. *Conversations With God (Pt. 1)*. New York: Penguin Putnam Young Reader, 1996.

Watts, Alan. *The Book*. New York: Vintage Books, 1989.

Wilber, Ken. *No Boundary*. Boston: Shambhala, 1985.

Young, Shinzen. *Five Classic Meditations*. New York: St. Martins, 1989.

Zinn, John Kabat. *Wherever You Go, There You Are*. New York: Hyperion, 1994.

Zukav, Gary. *The Dancing Wu Li Masters*. New York: Bantam Books, 1980.

INDEX

✦ ✦ ✦

Give the Gift of **No Bad Feelings!**
to Your Friends and Loved Ones

CHECK YOUR LEADING BOOKSTORE OR ORDER HERE
Web site: www.atlasbooks.com/marktplc/00613.htm
or www.NoBadFeelings.com

❏ **YES**, I want _____ copies of *No Bad Feelings!* at $12.95 each, plus $4 shipping per book (Colorado and Ohio residents please add $.91 sales tax per book). Canadian orders must be accompanied by a postal money order in U.S. funds. Allow 15 days for delivery.

❏ **YES**, I am interested in having June and Jim speak or give a seminar to my company, association, school, or organization. Please send information.

My check or money order for $_____ is enclosed.
Please charge my: ❏ Visa   ❏ MasterCard
                   ❏ Discover ❏ American Express

Name _____

Organization _____

Address _____

City/State/Zip _____

Phone_____ E-mail _____

Card # _____

Exp. Date_____ Signature _____

Please make your check payable and return to:
BookMasters, Inc.
P.O. Box 388 • Ashland, OH 44805

Call your credit card order to: 800-247-6553
Fax: 419-281-6883 • E-mail: order@bookmaster.com
✦ ✦ ✦
www.NoBadFeelings.com
www.atlasbooks.com/marktplc/00613.htm
**To contact the authors directly with your comments,
ideas or reviews, e-mail: LetGoandLiveLtd@aol.com**